T0067884

# Thirsting for More

## Writings from Sacred Center

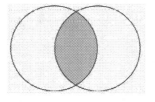

*with*

## Wendi Romero

| Library of Congress Control Number: | | 2022916378 |
| --- | --- | --- |
| ISBN: | Hardcover | 978-1-6698-4557-7 |
| | Softcover | 978-1-6698-4556-0 |
| | eBook | 978-1-6698-4555-3 |

Print information available on the last page.

Rev. date: 09/12/2022

**To order additional copies of this book, contact:**
Xlibris
844-714-8691
www.Xlibris.com
Orders@Xlibris.com
791926

# CONTENTS

*Let God work in you like a loving Mother. Then doors will open in walls where you didn't know there was a door. —Katherine Meeks, PhD.*

## Introduction

I sit in Honeysuckle Cottage, which should now be called, "Fern and Ivy Cottage," as the lush greenness of summer surrounds my home, and the ivy twines up to the door. As I cast my eyes back across the many years since Sacred Center was born, I understand more clearly that Soul will have its way; that it directs us in profound inner and outer journeys.

This new book, a gift of our journeys, has come together through time and prayer, in the long, slow process of arriving at our own truths. We walk through liminal space, the threshold of change, and we are given the wisdom needed for each new task. It might be Covid, or challenges in our families, or simply holding the profound struggles of this world we live in. This book has been birthed through challenge, struggle, and deep joy. We want to lift our voices as we grow and change.

Almost every author of note in the fields of spirituality and philosophy is insisting that the world desperately needs feminine energies as we consider the deep structural problems of our world. The feminine in both men and women knows how to share, to collaborate, to ponder, to cooperate, and to nurture. I think I felt this need years ago when I was filled with longing … for something. For a new way of being in the world. I was living largely through masculine energies that cause us to strive for production and success. Maybe many of us will do this in the first half of life, then our female soul wakes up and demands that we pay her attention. It was out of her voice that Sacred Center was born, and we began to come together.

I have discovered that when women do come together, as we have weekly at Sacred Center, and daily on our Facebook page, there is a Sacred Alchemy. When the feminine has its way, "doors open in walls where we didn't know there was a door." Time slows, and the joy of, "being," walks in. Barriers fall and love flows. The key is acceptance of each other as we are. We trust that change, if needed, comes from within. And we concentrate on our own journeys, our own inner lives, the love that we want to share.

Someday maybe I will write a book called, "Thursdays at 9:30." For now, I will just say that I am in my cottage every week at this time, and all comers are welcomed.

This is an open group that constantly changes. People come as they can and leave when they need to concentrate on other things, yet we stay connected. I hope that you, dear reader, enjoy coming into this space through reading this book, the soul-offering of your sisters, jewels found along the great path that we all walk together.

—Lyn Holley Doucet, Founder of Sacred Center

## About the Cover Art

We thirst for the living waters, poured lovingly and without hesitation by the three Marys who bore witness to the passing of the Christ. The three women and the Holy Trinity reflect one another, melting into each other in the waters of life that Mary offers from her vessel in one continuous and eternal moment. I was reminded of David Whyte's poem, "Where Many Rivers Meet," and how it captures the essence of the image created for this book, *Thirsting for More*.

All the water below me came from above.
All the clouds living in the mountains
gave it to the rivers,
who gave it to the sea, which was their dying.

And so I float on cloud become water,
central sea surrounded by white mountains,
the water salt, once fresh,
cloud fall and stream rush, tree root and tide bank,
leading to the rivers; mouths
and the mouths of the rivers sing into the sea,
the stories buried in the mountains
give out into the sea
and the sea remembers
and sings back, from the depths,
where nothing is forgotten.

I love the continuity of thirst for the holy and everflowing waters that are offered to us without hesitation. It is the story of the ongoing relationship between the human and the divine, the knowing that when we thirst for the Spirit, the Spirit flows like water into our parched hearts.

—Dana Manly, Artist

*When I drink it, the stream enters me.* —LL Barkat

**For the Reader**

Water is the essence of life, and our very survival depends on it. Everything in nature thirsts, and is constantly thirsting for more. The soul thirsts, too. The psalmist writes, "As a deer longs for streams of water, so my soul longs for you, O God. My soul thirsts for God, the living God." Psalm 42:2

Twelve years ago, I ran into Lyn Doucet, the founder of Sacred Center, in a coffee shop in Breaux Bridge, La. I knew her then as a local retreat leader, author, and spiritual director. I was just beginning to dip my toe in the flow of life again following a traumatic brain injury. After a brief conversation, she invited me to a "Soup and Story" event that she was hosting at her home. "Bring a short story and celery for the soup," she said. I accepted her invitation and showed up with a green stalk in one hand and an essay of a recent pilgrimage in the other. The aroma of the slowly boiling soup filled the room while twelve women told stories of love, loss, awakenings, and discoveries. It brought me alive again to be in the presence of women sharing vulnerably and authentically about the fabric of their lives. Then came the invitation to sit silently with this women's circle in centering prayer every Thursday morning. My deep thirst to fully engage in community again responded to that call, and before Sacred Center ever had a name, the women who showed up became a "holding place" for me while I was still healing. My responses were often delayed, I stuttered, and sometimes simply couldn't summon the words I wanted to speak. Their kindness, love, and compassion created a cushion of safety and warmth that helped facilitate my further healing. As my friend, Avis, wrote, "Divine guidance brought me here, Divine thirst and love kept me coming back."

Last summer my husband, Keith, cleared out what was left of our flower beds and took on the monumental task of redesigning and replanting a new landscape across the front of the house. The new blooms attracted many visitors to our yard—butterflies, dragonflies, hummingbirds, a few bees, and wasps, too. New life everywhere. This spring, while he was recovering from knee surgery, I was left with the responsibility of watering the flower beds every evening. What began as a chore soon became a time of serenity, peace, and contemplation for me. During the hottest days, the pentas and vincas seemed to never get enough water. While they were constantly drinking it in and thirsting for more, I began to sense my own divine thirst growing inside—an intense longing and thirst for God; seeking God where God could be found in my grief and pain, and also in the collateral beauty of life.

Barry Lopez, in his children's book, *Crow and Weasel,* writes through his character, Badger, that "stories people tell have a way of taking care of them. If stories come to you, care for them. And learn to give them away where they are needed. Sometimes a person needs a story more than food to stay alive." I think we also have an unquenchable thirst for such stories to sustain us, especially when we find ourselves spiritually in a dry, parched, and barren land.

This book is filled with many stories and poems of love and loss, faith and doubt, courage and trust, hope and joy. These are the real lives of real women who have gathered every Thursday morning for the last twelve years to share, listen, and hold what life had to offer. In our previous book, *Reflections of the Heart,* Lyn wrote, "these writings come from places that have been drenched with living water."

The stories and poems in this book are grouped according to themes. This is a book that doesn't require reading straight through from beginning to the end. You can start somewhere in the middle if you'd like, or if the Spirit is leading you to a particular topic on any given day. Read one poem or story a day or read an entire section; but most importantly, it is our hope that you take quiet time afterward to reflect on what is rising up in you. You may come to recognize similar themes in your own life. There is a question following each writing that serves as a prompt for you to do your own writing. A journal would be helpful to record your thoughts or bring your own images to life. You may feel the desire to write your own poem or short story, paint or draw, go for a long walk, a bike ride, or water your flower garden. Whatever helps to move your thoughts or feelings from the inside out, that you might hear what Love and Wisdom from within wants to offer you.

For many years, most of us sit at the feet of those we highly regard as spiritual teachers. When we remove all distractions and sit with intention and an open heart, we can each hear the voice of the Divine for ourselves. Sometimes, it's a whisper or a nudge, and sometimes it's as loud and clear as thunder. As the well-loved author, poet, and spiritual teacher, Macrina Wiederkehr once said, "Now is the time for me to sit at my own feet and listen to what the Spirit is saying to me."

These stories and poems are sacred to this circle of women, "care for them and give them away where they are needed." As you drink from the stream of our lives, allow it to enter you. May it water your own life and leave you thirsting for more. Go slowly. Drink deeply.

—Wendi Romero, Editor

*I too have taken myself into this summer lake where peace comes in the generosity of water. I have reached out into the loveliness to think out a poem or two, not by any means fluid but, dear God, as you have made me, my only quickness. —Mary Oliver*

**Thirst**

In a world
that seems to
divide us

more than
unite us,
*Now* is

the time for
a greater Love,
a love that is

constantly
being poured
out upon us.

All we must
do is
thirst for it.

—Wendi Romero

# Awakenings and Discoveries

Photo by Wendi Romero

*Everything you see has its roots in the unseen world. The forms change yet the essence remains the same.* —*Rumi*

## Lifting the Veil

Wander in wonder, behold in awe: the Beloved awaits.
Turn toward beauty and find Home.

—Deidre Montgomery

*For your reflection:* Where is home?

*This is love, to fly toward a secret sky. In the end, to take a step without feet. —Rumi*

**It's Not Too Late**

It is raining outside, and I am playing "Maple Leaf Rag" on the piano. It is a simplified version, but it has much of the jazzy feeling and rocking beat of the original. To play a song is to get inside it in a way that simply listening cannot do. It's a trip into the composer's mind and motivations. And also, playing "Maple Leaf Rag" just for myself, is a lot of fun.

I have "played at" piano much of my life. I took piano as a child, and then fifteen years ago, after I learned chord theory on the guitar, I began to play the piano by the chord method. I could read music, but not well enough. I wanted to read better, know more, and play more skillfully.

So, two years ago, I began taking weekly lessons. It is one of the best things I ever did for myself. I am, by far, the oldest student at Acadiana Music Academy. But I don't mind that at all. I love my teacher, Angel, who is thirty. She and I are very simpatico, and she is warm and encouraging, not scary as my childhood teacher was. I am progressing rather slowly, I think, but I am progressing. Every once in a while, I surprise myself with what I can do now.

But this isn't really an essay about playing the piano. It's a tale about how it's never too late to do what we wished we had done. Another example in my life is that I returned to school when I was in my fifties to become a licensed professional counselor. Counseling is probably what I always should have done. I love it; it's what I am interested in.

I say these things not because I am so wonderful but because folks give up too soon. We can box ourselves in without good reason. I often see this in my counseling practice; we heed the words of others who say we're too old, or that if we haven't done it yet, we never will, and so on. And we listen to our own inner critic. We can be left feeling that we don't have the feet to take that first step, but this is an illusion of fear, nothing else.

3

I write this knowing that I am a privileged person and financially secure. Many are not. But often fear or shame are much bigger barriers than finances in pursuing a dream, even a small one. It doesn't have to be this way. If we want to paint, we can get some supplies and begin, or take a class. If we want to write, we can pick up a pen or type on our laptops. If we want to do that 5-K or something more challenging, let's put on those shoes and get started. And it's not too late to return to school. Most universities have special departments to help older students. Start with one class. At the very least—and it's not a small thing—you will make new friends.

Sometimes we stay mired in the lives of others, trying to fix their problems, when we might be a better example by getting on with life ourselves. Doing what we've always wanted to do. It's really not too late. And doing something new, having a beginner's mind, and holding humility in both hands—well, it's refreshing. It's life giving. There is always something to learn, some new door in the mind to be opened. We don't have to pretend to know everything, no matter how old we are.

We needn't show the world our efforts, and certainly not our initial ones. I don't plan to give concerts. But in the early morning hours, when the house is quiet and I am sipping my coffee and playing, "You Are Mine," as written, with the key change to five sharps, I am pleased. I am flowing with life in a different way; I am flying toward my own secret sky.

—Lyn Holley Doucet

*For your reflection*: Consider ordering a copy of The Artist's Way by Julia Cameron or check your library. You can get an inexpensive used copy if you like. This book has meant so much to me and inspired me in many ways.

## Dropped at My Door

On occasion I come across a word or a phrase that inspires me to write. The phrase that follows is one such starter: dropped at my door ...

It's a cool dry morning, especially for the beginning of May in the Deep South. The red planet is sinking below the oaks;

stars litter the five a.m. sky. It is still and dark, that darkness just before dawn. The quiet is broken only by the sound of crickets

and a lone rooster in the distance. Nary a mosquito is seen, heard, or felt, so unusual after all of the recent rains we've had.

I shiver a little in the coolness and wrap a blanket around myself, a little cocoon, as I wait. The birds begin to wake, greeting the

morning. The sky lightens as I sip tea. My breath is soft and even as I sink further into my chair, relaxed but waiting for the next

thing to reveal itself. The trees that were as dark as pencil sketches begin to show bits of color: grey-green leaves,

black branches showing bits of brown. The sunlight begins to peek over the eastern sky to my back and adds more light; color

begins to show itself in the landscape of my backyard. Grey and black sketches become watercolor paintings as more light

penetrates the sky; blues and greens and browns begin to differentiate themselves, and gold highlights sparkle off of shiny

leaves and blades of grass. Bird songs begin to fill the air; occasionally I see the singers as they flitter among the oaks.

I catch a glimpse of a squirrel scampering from branch to branch. Traffic noises begin as folks journey to work and school.

I am aware of movement and noise. It feels as if peace has dropped at my door. I breathe it in; it becomes prayer, an Alleluia.

—Trudy Gomez

*For your reflection*: Try to recall when a phrase you encountered led to further discovery.

*A journey becomes a pilgrimage as we discover, day by day, that the distance traveled is less important than the experience gained.*
*—Ernest Kurtz*

## Pilgrimage

I learned much later that it was the swan dance, the swooped-neck poetry in motion, that had the pilgrims farther up the road mesmerized. I was so curious to see what they were seeing, to experience what they were experiencing, but had lost ground with every step they took. My body was caving in under me and I could no longer keep up with the pack. All the while, I'm aware of every single breath I deeply draw and every burning step that moves me slowly along. I hear Joseph, a fellow pilgrim who stayed behind with me, say "breathe in earth, blow out fire."

I trudged under the weight of my backpack and over the ooze of breaking blisters on the soles of my feet. Even though I'd lost sight of everyone else, it no longer mattered, because I was forging my own path now. I looked up and saw the moon and star on the bell towers of the cathedral high in the sky over Chartres, France. Instead of the group leader, those symbols now serve as my compass. I'm not lost and I know they will point me in the right direction.

This was my second walking pilgrimage from Paris to Chartres in the spring of 2009. The path we were on was a portion of one of the routes of the Camino de Santiago de Compostela, the "way of the stars" that leads to the Cathedral of St. James in Santiago, Spain. My first pilgrimage in 2007 had presented a few small challenges which I easily overcame. But in those two years, I had been through menopause, sustained a head injury, and undergone a rhinoplasty and sinus surgery. My intentions were in the right place, and I felt like my body had fully recovered, and that I was strong enough to endure the journey, so I thought. But, life had something else in store. The path unfolded as it did, in a way I could have never expected nor imagined.

Many roads winded and twisted their way to the old city of Chartres. On the first trip, we walked a forty-five mile path on foot from the south of Paris through lush poppy fields, pea gravel and cement. The surface was often shifting, but I managed to adjust easily along the way. This time, a hot, turning, and uneven road of asphalt was the last few miles of the journey. Consumed by the fire I felt in my feet, I had no idea what awaited me at the next bend or how much further I would have to go. By now, I'm thinking that the other fifteen pilgrims have surely arrived, laid down their backpacks, and are marveling before the grand entrance of the magnificent cathedral.

I lagged way behind and arriving with my fellow pilgrims wasn't in the cards this time. This was *my* pilgrimage, and I would arrive in my own slow time. As I looked up from the weight of my world and the heaviness of my belongings, I saw two familiar faces sitting on a green bench. When they saw me, it was as if the angels had rushed to meet me. One of them offered to carry my backpack, but I didn't easily relinquish it.

I had packed it and felt that this baggage was mine alone to carry. Still, there was more walking and more lessons to be learned on this path. I finally agreed to let them lighten my load by carrying a few of my t-shirts and an extra pair of walking shoes. They slowed their own rhythms to keep pace with mine.

As we passed a school playground, I realized I was severely dehydrated. Gulps of water and a surge of endorphins came to my aid. The sounds of children at play were distant, but so familiar to me. I watched them, as if in slow motion, while some other part of me was being awakened from a long deep sleep. One of the kid's balls landed at my feet, and I summoned the energy to kick it back. The same ball landed in front of me a second time, and once more I kicked it back. While I listened to out-of-breath six year olds converse in French about a game of kick-ball, I could sense my own six year old "inner child" showing up—the little girl that used to dream, play, and converse in the same native tongue. Memories of images and sounds of my old neighborhood, my first home in southwest Louisiana, began to stir.

Long buried beneath a brain injury, pieces of my parents' first language and my upbringing deep in the heart of Acadian French country, began to resurrect. This "remembering" could only happen in a language that my inner child could understand. That day on the hot cement road to Chartres, France, I was transported across a sea of time and an ocean of experiences.

Today, I'm deeply grateful for both my Acadian French and French mainland heritage, upon which the foundation of my life has been built. My migrant ancestors were a people of strong resolve and deep spirituality, memorialized and celebrated to this very day. I still feel the fire.

—Wendi Romero

*For your reflection*: Recall a time when an outer event awakened your inner roots. What awareness did it bring you to?

*Do not break faith with your awakened heart.* —*James Finley*

**Navigating These Changing Times**

This phrase of James Finley's vibrated within me with a similar vibration when I read the title of a 2000 Dawna Markova book, *I Will Not Die an Unlived Life*. I didn't know how they were connected, but both captured a place in my being that felt linked somehow.

Perhaps the link is that my awakened heart opened me to seeking direction for my life, and that book title was the reminder to keep moving on the path to awareness. I already felt, like so many of my generation and gender, that there might be more to life than what I was showing up for or than was showing up for me. An investigation was called for. James Finley's words, heard only days ago, and that book title from years past jumped into my heart, linking. I think the connection can be explained in his further statement about the awakened heart.

James Finley spoke of the way spirit speaks to us and how silence is a big part of putting ourselves into a position for guidance and of always being willing to course correct. He said, and I paraphrase, listen for words or other promptings of your heart, look to nature for guidance, listen for the encouragement of your guides on how to live your life. This is where the two join for me. Available to me are all these ways in which I can learn to live my life. I have nature as an example; I have other people to look to and I find guidance in so many places.

Awakening and age have placed a greater drive to make my life count, if only to me. Guidance is available, and I want a life lived, the link. I know I've always had the great desire to live my life fully, I just sometimes forgot or broke faith with it as I was distracted in other directions.

Today is my birthday. It is a beautiful spring day in May, cool and sunny. I am sheltering in place at home with my husband. I have the company of squirrels and birds, lizards and salamanders, various bugs; all visitors to our yard and an occasional snake (shudder). The garden is producing huge red tomatoes, green beans, peppers, chard, beets, zucchini, butternut squash, corn, and I am probably missing some things. The herb beds are flourishing. I am particularly enjoying holy basil as tea, such a nice fresh taste and the phrase, "Summer time and the livin' is easy"comes to mind. It feels easy from this vantage point. I know it isn't easy for so very many people.

Back to James Finley's quote. In this time of Covid-19, we are all finding that we are having to course correct in so many areas. The whole planet is being asked to course correct, and many of us are struggling for guidance but, there are many who do look to nature, look to guides, and look to our inner strength to make "easy livin" more available. I realize that I am fortunate in that I don't have to rely on a job for pay, and I have a comfortable home and I am not hungry or without resources. I also have many people whom I care for and who care about me. Life is easier for me than for so many. I am aware of that and I don't forget it. I am enormously grateful.

I have been sheltered since the end of February, and I am still okay with it, but I would like a little more interaction, especially family gatherings. I do have lovely company visiting in the yard from time to time, and that is appreciated greatly. I suppose we will venture out a little in the next few weeks. We aren't even going inside grocery stores at this time, relying on curbside pick-up options which are so convenient. I do miss choosing my own groceries but not enough to forego the caution, not yet. We both fit into several of the "at risk" categories, so we have been cautious.

The muse, even the desire to write, has been elusive for me and I find for others as well, having spoken to many of my friends on the subject. I find it to be curious considering the very strange and extraordinary time in which we are living. It would seem we would be getting it all down on paper; maybe we will with hindsight musings.

I'm not even sure how to chronicle the events now, they are too immeasurable. How do you speak about this thing without that thing and then this other thing? How do you even put together such strange comparisons and contrasts to what was before? The magnitude is overwhelming if I take in the whole of it. I can't seem to take in any of it except by getting up in the morning, and how do we do this day and then this evening and they seem to be very much alike, one after the other. I think I am more present to my moments now than I ever remember being. It sounds boring but it isn't. I find it to be relaxing; no hurry, no rush to get anything done except the two meals on the table; we both like scheduled times in our day.

When I consider what to write about at this time and I begin to think beyond my place in the whole of this, I realize that I can't know how another is experiencing this time. They tell me the actions of their day and even their frustrations, anxieties, and their joys, opportunities and hopes; I still don't know, not really, all the emotions that arise and subside, that activate and calm because we can never truly experience another's experience.

It is when things have strayed into the realm of avoiding my life, and it happens, I am called back to James Finley and Dawna Markova. I am called back to their words when I am feeling blue or deprived. I am called back to their words when I realize that I have so many advantages and that I have a responsibility to support those who need to be held and prayed for and loved in this time. Those who need to be accepted and not judged, who need to be heard whether I agree or not. This is such a very strange time. The way to capture the essence of this will be ascertained in hindsight and for many years, I think.

One of the things that I am slowly, gradually learning is that I don't want to engage with the angry voices, or the hatred, or the division. When I am reading something that goes there, I do my very best to not engage in that. I don't always succeed, but my awareness of it is so acute that I am getting much better at it. I think that might be one of the greater lessons of this time. We need to be in harmony. Coming together for unity and making good decisions for all is critical for our living an awakened life. Being us and we; not they or them.

—Avis Lyons LeBlanc

*For your reflection:* Can you go to love when you see others go to hate, or fear, or anger? Can you open your heart for holding the sacred?

12

*So can dreams change someone's life? Of course they can.*
—*Stanley Krippner*


## The Initiation of Dreams

For a couple of years recently, I worked seriously with my night dreams. Kate Burns, a Jungian analyst from Houston, Tx, and I collaborated by phone in ninety-minute sessions of interpretation that left me breathless with wonder.

Kate advised me that I was undergoing an initiation, deep within, a soul healing and change. I felt like a heroine on a mystic quest in the darkness of the night; I was in search of my true self.

The more I wrote my dreams down, the more I remembered them. It was as though the inner dreamer said, "Oh, you're taking this seriously? I am going to help you remember!" As time passed, I became more and more convinced that we miss great help for our lives when we ignore our dreams.

In June of 2019 (close to my birthday), I had this deeply luminous dream:

I am taken to a closet and asked to pick out a garment. I choose a beautiful, white, embroidered dress which I put on. I am taken to a round, shallow pool filled with water.

In this baptism dream, the lovely white dress is a symbol of both purity and spirituality. During the baptism ceremony the old self is left behind and a new, spiritually cleansed self is invoked. I was in touch with what I was leaving behind: the many graspings of my ego. In their place was the birthing of deep compassion for myself and others. A willingness to suffer when needed and yet a tangible knowing that life is good. I was releasing my expectations and accepting life as it is; becoming more flexible about my plans and desires and more tender about the needs of others. I could see my faults more clearly, and I was less sensitive to criticism. I was okay with being a work in progress.

This dream came, with its beautiful imagery, as a balm, to heal and to encourage. It filled me up with grace.

The poet, Kahlil Gibran, writes, "The soul walks not upon a line, neither does it grow like a reed. The soul unfolds itself, like a lotus of countless petals."

In dreamwork, the soul unfolds her petals and shows herself as beautiful, wise, and rich with meaning. Nightly she asks that we receive her.

As I write this today, I decide to make a collage of this dream. The dress in the dream is very much like a wedding dress. (The symbology of marriage in a dream is profound and a writing for another day.) A picture of a wedding dress should be relatively easy to find. Perhaps a woman with her back to the camera, one in contemplation, close to a pool of the bluest water. It's time, once again, to celebrate this dream because it continues to unfold in my life.

—Lyn Holley Doucet

*For your reflection:* Consider putting a pen and pad beside your bed to record your dreams when you awake. Just seek to do this for one week. Then you can decide if you will continue. Don't rush to analyze your dreams, and don't use dream books (most aren't that helpful). Play with the images in your dreams, or write about them, and see what they mean to you.

# Celebration and Gratitude

Photo by Trudy Gomez

*If the sight of the blue skies fills you with joy, if a blade of grass springing up in the fields has the power to move you, if the simple things of nature have a message that you understand, rejoice for your soul is alive. —Eleanora Duse*

## Chrysalis

Once upon a moment, a cricket catches my eye and jumps in the high grass of the turn row.

Thus, my first seeing as a conscious presence of God. Sitting on my patio swing, I watch a lizard devour a bug. I see a flitting monarch taste the nectar of the blue Plumbago flower while two squirrels play chase up, down, and around the tree. Two hawks fly high overhead, and the song of cicadas fills the air, penetrating the depths of my ears.

I am in this moment—fully aware. THIS is peace.

My view of the distant tree line, now almost obscured by growing sugarcane, will soon disappear completely. The circling hawk calls out to its unseen mate. A blue jay descends from a branch to capture a June bug from my flowerbed while the sound of cicadas drones on. For this cool summer morning, I give praise and thanks to You, O God. My red shrimp plant has returned from its near-death experience. Pruning it to the root of its life gave it a new beginning; thus, my last-ditch effort to save it proved effective.

From lack comes life! Thank You, Lord, for your amazing grace.

My yellow shrimp plant grows tall with a bounty of leaves. Two strong yellow flowers have stood tall for weeks, and eleven buds are expected to bloom just as beautifully. My pink Peace rose peeks out from behind the squirrel feeder, while the Turk's Cap flowers glimmer in the soft breeze, like a drape of red Christmas lights shining on the tall leafy-stemmed bush. The stem of a pink Gaura bends as a lizard leaps from its perch on the fence to capture a bug or, perhaps searching for one. The breeze is ever so gentle over me.

18

My life is full and my joy is with You. I am your creature in the garden of Love.

My two-year-old Bleeding Heart is finally blooming. I'm so proud and happy to see the red and white clusters hang sporadically from the branches of my Astilbe. Patience and trust are virtues.

I walk through my yard, picking up branches and twigs downed from the recent Louisiana rainstorm. Grass, trees, sugarcane – all plants lifting up their limbs, leaves, and branches in thanksgiving and praise for His life-giving water. A dragonfly flits from grass to plants, searching for sustenance.

Such a beautiful, delicate creature seasoning my joy.

A crow flies toward the tree line, cawing, as though goading another to see who will get there first—only to land on a branch ever so briefly, then fly about again.

Hark! A pause, a moment of stillness. Like a breath being held, there is no breeze. The sugarcane stands motionless like a field of sentinels. No birds, no squirrels, no movement but for the ceiling fan overhead. I hear the soft cawing of crows in the distance. I enjoy a wonderful reprieve from the piercing sound of cicadas.

Peace. Be still. Know that I am God.

Suddenly, life stirs up again. Two hawks, two squirrels, and a blue jay break from the stillness.

A yellow butterfly flits in and out between rows of sugarcane. Living in the present is so new to me. The message now hangs on the door of my heart: "Be aware! Pay close attention!" Behind the door of my heart lies the secret to becoming my authentic self: Live consciously in the presence of God.

Thank you, Lord, for this beautiful gift of seeing with new eyes.

You lifted the veil for this beautiful moment in time.

The dark ghostly shadow of a silent crow flying high above moves stealthily across the tall grass in the sunlit turn-row. White puffy clouds sit low and unmoving in a blue-grey sky. Cicadas sing their song in the ebb and flow of a low key. Grass grows, a butterfly flits about, a leaf falls. All is well. God lives in me.

I name the door to my heart "Chrysalis!"

—Velma LeBlanc Cheramie

*For your reflection:* What messages are spoken to you when you are out in God's creation? Journal about these things today.

*Awareness is like the sun. When it shines on things, they are transformed. —Thich Nhat Hanh*

**Sometimes It's Simple**

Sometimes, it's as simple
as sitting on a stump
and seeing how slanted
light falls golden on
a spinning fetch of
dancing dragonflies.

Sometimes, it's as simple
as bending an ear to
an encircling whir of
a swirling swarm of
flying mystics
hovering around.

Sometimes, it's as simple
as gazing at
the intricate design
of a delicate
bug-eyed creature
destined for flight.

Sometimes, in a thin space
we gain a momentary glimpse
of transparent wings
departing outer skin,
rising and sailing
on currents of wind.

—Wendi Romero

***For your reflection***: May you be aware of the simple things.

## Oasis

Shimmer
Mirage or reality?
Draws you in
Draws you deeper
Light changes
Perspective changes
Does light shift or do I?
See the ordinary become extraordinary!

How often do I go around in a daze,
Blind to the things around me?
So narrow is my vision;
Blinded by just getting by
Just getting through
One foot in front of the other
Going through the motions.

Spirit residing within
Beckoning,
Calling and shimmering like an oasis,
Drawing me in
Penetrating my heart.
Listening to Spirit saying
"Come be refreshed
Be renewed."
Drawing me deeper
Light changes
Perspective changes
Does light shift or do I?
See the ordinary become extraordinary!

—Trudy Gomez

*For your reflection:* Allow yourself to be refreshed and renewed by resting in the presence of Spirit.

*Inspired by Isaiah 49 and Psalm 62*

## Untitled Reflection

He said:
I hold you in the palm of my hand,
You are held in love.
I love you in your messiness,
In your negativity and your cynicism.
You are enough!

He said:
When you have no self-love,
I love you.
When you have no self-appreciation,
I love you.
You are enough!

He said:
I Am bigger than what you can contain.
I Am more expansive than you can conceive.
In my breath is love, joy, compassion.
I Am the abundance that surrounds you.
I Am the source of your freedom.

He said:
I hold you in the palm of my hand,
Allow the embrace,
Allow the love,
Allow the peace,
You are enough!

—Trudy Gomez

*For your reflection*: Read Isaiah 49 and Psalm 62.

## Rise

Rise up, oh life, from ashes thought to be dust
turned into newness as the seasons turn.
Drawn within the darkness, silent sleep
recreates from the essence of before.

Breaking out and breaking through as does a seed
or a winged creature from cocoon,
whatever was before is forever changed,
disillusion washed away in renewal.

Light stretches longer into each day,
illuminating what was once thought lost.
Rise, and rise again from yesterday's fall,
a new hope like never known before.

Now waiting fills, the unknown is known.
Questions rise into the mystery,
giving forth a knowledge, giving forth
a new unknowingness together.

What was broken once again is whole,
clothed in new garments of radiance.
What was once lost, again is found.
Rejoice in the joy of reunion!

Rise again, oh Joy, rise again!
Greet the dawn with anticipation
in the fullness of all that is all!
Rise, new life, and fill the world anew.

—B. D. Lowry

*For your reflection*: I rise anew, with new hope for the world.

## You Are a Treasure, a Pearl Beyond Price

In prayer this morning, these words came: You are a pearl beyond price. I cover each of your imperfection with my grace and mercy. You are luminescent! Surrender to compassion, surrender to love. What an invitation!

I always viewed Jesus as the pearl beyond price, the treasure. Then one day I asked the question, what if we are viewed in the same manner, that we are the pearl beyond price, the precious treasure? I think we must be, otherwise why would God have offered his Son for us; why would Jesus' life be sacrificed in order to give us life if we were not precious?

When a pearl is formed in nature, the oyster responds to an irritating foreign body by covering it in layers of the same substance produced by the oyster to make its shell. Layer after layer, until it is no longer recognized as a foreign body, it is part of the oyster! So too with us if we allow God to work in us and surround us; there comes a point that we are so covered in God's mercy and grace that we are no longer recognizable as what we were before. We are transformed into a glorious new creation; we are luminescent.

How could I not be thankful to Compassion, to Love! How can I not believe that I am God's treasure!

—Trudy Gomez

*For your reflection:*
Hear the words:
You are my pearl beyond price
I cover each of your imperfections
With grace
With mercy
You are luminescent!
You are my treasure!
Surrender to Compassion,
Surrender to Love.
What if you allowed?

What if you believed?
Why can't you let profound Love in?
Are you afraid of Love's power?
Do you think yourself deserving of it?
Are you afraid of the transformation that can take place?
Would you recognize yourself as glorious and precious?

# Community and Caring

Photo by Denise Broussard

*As parents age, sometimes their children become caretakers.*

## Apple Pie and My Mother-In-Law

I had never paid much attention to her until I met her son. Apple pie was the first food she offered me when her son brought me home to officially meet her. She served me apple pie topped with a dollop of vanilla ice-cream, a combination I had never eaten before! The warm and cold combination of the dessert was wonderful!

Desserts eaten, I picked up her son's saucer and spoon along with mine to bring them to the kitchen, for that was what my mother had taught the girls in our home. "Love him through the stomach, pick the dishes up, and clean them!"

His mother was impressed! He was impressed! He told me that no other girl had ever done that for him! He told me later that he knew we'd be married. At the time, I was certain only that he was trying to go steady with me! After three dates, we were thinking alike! He and I were meant to be together! Fourteen months later, he was my husband, and she was my mother-in-law! And I have loved her as family since the apple pie!

Today, she lives with my husband and me, her caretakers. She was diagnosed with Alzheimer's disease nearly six years ago. Her body is strong; she never was sickly. Many days she lies there sleeping peacefully and we care for her. Some days are good days: she smiles and offers us kisses, especially her son and me and our daughter! Some days she stares at the ceiling and smiles. I wonder whom she sees.

And she still loves sweets, like apple pie and ice-cream!

—Cheryl Delahoussaye

*For your reflection*: Think about what being a caretaker might be like for you.

*The important people in our lives leave imprints. They may stay or go but they are always in our hearts. —Rachel Cohn*

**A Rare Find**

It's a rare find,
a priceless jewel,
when one comes
along as a ray of
bright light shining
on the different
facets of life

where words need
not be measured
nor thoughts
second-guessed.
Where presence
is true joy and
cause for celebration,

where there is a soft
place to land when
life's lessons grow hard.
Many pass our way
but few come across
our lives to stay
and change us
forever.

—Wendi Romero

***For your reflection***: Remember those who have left an imprint on your life.

*When we hold space we make more room in our hearts so that others can be in theirs. —Helen Avery*

**Holding Space**

Holding space—
opening to life
like cupped hands
held side by side

where presence,
with a deep surrender
to what is,
holds all the power.

A bridge of compassion
to and from stories
that break and
remake us,

where blood flows
between the two
and hearts beat
as one.

Only a river of space
between us,
a container
without borders,

a vessel of hope
in the midst
of a raging
storm.

No fixing,
just being with.
Holding space …
a holding place.

—Wendi Romero

*For your reflection*: Sometimes all you need to do is simply hold space.

## Fragile

The cycling of life,
letting go of my notions of how things should be,
facing how things are,
the great circle of life.

In it, I am a fragile one, the one holding on,
the vulnerable one feeling lost in a mist.
I am cradled in my fragility
by the circle that enfolds me with grace
and acceptance and wisdom.
My fragility shared and understood by wise ones.

I sit in a place
tears allowed to flow,
soft words comfort
shared laughter lifts.
I am touched by grace;
breath and body
held in God's tender embrace

—Trudy Gomez

*For your reflection:* Do you have people in your life who cradle you
when you are feeling fragile?

*Though one may be overpowered, two can defend themselves. A cord of three strands is not quickly broken. —Ecclesiastes 4:12*

## Cord of Three Strands

In faithful and true friendships,
Issues that should not matter.
What country you're from,
What language you speak,
What color your skin,
What traditions you follow.

Individuals with different personalities,
Different lifestyles, different friendships,
Different beliefs, different religions …
All beloved children of God.

One common denominator,
The third cord binding us together.
Our Father in heaven,
Our confidante and companion.

Unlike family relationships
that are not chosen by us,
We can choose to enter into
marriage, partnerships,
and friendships.

Humans want someone to talk to,
Someone to share ideas, dreams,
joys and a shoulder to cry on.
Someone to depend on with presence
or trusting they are praying for you.

Someone to enjoy being around,
accepting all that you are.
Someone who shares values

on important things,
just letting the little things be.

Think of all the things we have to do.
We work, clean, and prepare meals.
We take care of our families, kids, and parents.
Friends choose to do things for each other.

Friendships should be a relationship
with no strings attached.
No expectations but one—
Just being there as best as you can,
Each totally accepting that fact.

I'm blessed to stay in touch
with old friends.
I continue to make new ones
as I move through the world.
Friends bound together
in Christ are stronger.

Many choose to live and work alone.
Wisdom says two are better than one.
In a difficult situation, three are even better.

—Denise Broussard

*For your reflection*: Have you found true friends that are bound
together as faithful as your friend, Jesus? Do you accept and love them
unconditionally for who they are, nothing more, nothing less?

*We adopted our son, and he and his birth mother met.*

### The Gift of Two Mothers

I was one of these two mothers, and I always wondered what she might look like, but I loved her for the gift she had given to my husband and me.

I was encouraged by our priest to pray for her. I often prayed especially on the days that were important: his birthday, a day she may have last seen him, the days she may have wondered what became of him. I chose March 7, the day we received him. I prayed she would not worry and that her heart would be settled that he was well taken care of.

Her gift to me was a gift from God. Her gift would always be a wonder, with many questions for the two of us. Where? When? How? Might it happen one day that there would be a gathering to learn about the past?

After forty-two years there was! All met: the boy, now man, and the two mothers.

The day we met was in a southern Louisiana park, with some members of the two families. Our son introduced us, the two mothers. We hugged, and cried, and laughed, and held each other and thanked one another!

For a while, both felt as if we were the only two present in time. Then there was laughter; there were some answered questions; there was more thanksgiving; there were pictures; and these two women knew God had connected them in time in the one way that only HE could!

—Cheryl Delahoussaye

*For your reflection:* How would you have felt witnessing this reunion?

**I Move Over Your Soul**

Most recently I've become aware.
It turns out to become aware enlists
more awareness.

Periods at the end of my sentences dot
themselves. Exclamation marks hop out of
my pen like children dropping from a tree's branch.

I'm aware I have a new love for you, my husband.
It's spawned from our old love. Not suddenly,
the way our first love came.

This new one is spawned incrementally, hour to hour,
day to day, and now decades are able to lean into us
with a shoulder of an azure blue grace,

like the sound loons make on a spring chilled lake;
their call, come here, come to me,
let's swim together as one.

Our earlier decades, I moved over your body, strong,
taut, supple, alive. Now I move over your soul
and your soul says: Come to me and I do.

I am aware of this shoulder of grace
like the sound loons make when
they call each other.

—Sidney Creaghan

*For your reflection:* Take the time to imagine the most meaningful
relationship in your life. Through writing or coloring, illuminate the
shoulder of grace between each of you.

# Darkness and Shadow

Photo by Wendi Romero

*Let's play "hide and seek" like the sun and the moon. We will hide so one of us can shine. —Harsha Jha*

## Hide and Seek

Words spoken between two lovers in the darkness of the bedroom. Words spoken around a campfire on a moonless night.

Words whispered in the darkness of the confessional, seeking forgiveness and a new beginning.

Words spoken by Nicodemus in the dead of night as he fought the fear of being discovered.

Words whispered in prayer as one struggles with the ghost of insomnia.

Words whispered by children as they play "hide and seek."

They seek those who hide in plain sight. They count to ten, some deliberately slow, others with rapid excitement: "1, 2, 3, 4, 5, 6, 7, 8, 9, 10 ... Ready or not, here I come!"

We search for those hidden in dark places: in a closet, under a bed, behind closed doors. Our hearts race at the anticipation of finding the hidden one.

Emotions of excitement and dread battle one another. When the game ends with shouts of joy and relief. We no longer fear being frightened. We relish in the joy of our reunion.

Words spoken in the dark are often the truest ever spoken. Things hidden, when they come to light, set us free. And I wonder, why do we fear the dark? What are we seeking?

—Patty Prather

*For your reflection*: "Olly, olly, open free," shouted at the end of children's "hide and seek" game means that those who were not found can come out into the open without losing the game. When have you heard God's voice calling you out of your fears and into a reunion with Him?

*God, give me grace to accept with serenity the things I cannot change,*
*courage to change the things I can, and wisdom to know the difference.*
*—Reinhold Niebuhr*

## As It Was, As It Is, As It Will Be

As it was,
we were moving
too damned fast,
hurrying from one place
to the next.

Bullet trains and jets,
broad-band internet,
global-access phones,
bitcoin and digital wallets,
planes clogging airspace.

Heads down, not looking
at where we're going,
our daily lives
totally consumed
by screens of all sizes.

Ears plugged with cutting
edge technology,
the need for speed, and more
instant gratification
has created addicts of us all.

As it is,
life turned on us,
spreading us out
and slowing us down to
an abrupt halt overnight.

Wiped-out grocery shelves,
frantic hysteria over
essential items,
empty church pews
and lonely highways;

crowded intensive care units,
where our mothers,
fathers and sisters,
brothers are all dying
from what we cannot see.

Our spiritual lives
sometimes take a back seat,
then come into focus again
when our familiar fades
and we no longer feel safe.

Long solitary walks
where mother nature
shakes me into
this fierce reality have
become my new normal,

turning my head that
I might see thorns among
the blackberries, the night
of the chrysalis before
the flight of the monarch,

and a southern magnolia,
curled so tightly
in the bud
about to break
open with hope.

As it will be
depends on us,
our response to
this one and only
gift of life.

Whatever the reason
for this pandemic,
this timeout, this period
of deep reflection,
it has our attention.

As apart as we are,
we're in it together.
It's time to wake-up,
lift our heads,
open our eyes,

and correct our vision,
that we might truly
see this space
and time as sacred.
How do we keep it that way?

—Wendi Romero

*For your reflection:* Where do you turn when life turns on you?

*What has been will be again. What has been done will be done again.*
*—Ecclesiastes 1:9*


## Feeling Tired

When I admit I'm feeling tired, it doesn't mean I want to give up. It doesn't mean that I'm not strong in the Lord. I simply feel tired. Subtle signs of aging, I assume. As much as we try to care for ourselves, my body, like all bodies, is subject to wear and tear. Tired muscles, achy joints, little patience, zapped energy to name a few. No one is immune. How I show up for these challenges makes all the difference in the world. Being mindful, I work on acceptance, openness, and being gentle with myself. The last thing I want is to feel resentment, anger, overwhelmed, or fearful of the aging process, which to a certain extent, I have no control over.

Thirty-eight years ago, God truly pulled me out of a pit of despair and set my feet on solid ground. I look back and see how I could have taken a much different path in life after losing my husband all those years ago. Somehow, some way, I made that leap of faith and followed the cross. I was so young, feeling tired even back then, but my Lord held me through those times and continues to do so to this day.

Worldly success was not important, so I retired when I was needed by loved ones. I said yes to a life of caregiving. I would think that those who have worked all of their lives and are close to reaching retirement age get tired too. With enough time invested, the desires and passions are not as strong as when they were younger. Caregiving for this many years is no different.

In my journal one morning I wrote, "I'm tired, my Lord." The very next day, in my reading, He sent me what I needed. "In those times when repetitive tasks begin to feel tiring, may we take a moment to offer each task to God as an offering of love." This statement spoke volumes to my heart, and I thanked Him for sending it. This one sentence made me shift my thinking about everything I do. Whether it's job related, caregiving, washing loads of clothes, washing dishes, car-pooling, mowing the yard, the list is endless of the many things we do automatically on a daily basis. All done as an offering of love just has a nice ring to it. It changed my human perspective to that of Jesus.'

I know in my heart there is value in every single thing I do. I ask Jesus to help me find joy in the many issues that keep me busy. When I focus on Him, he soothes me with his compassion to ease my heart's fatigue. I might stay busy, but I learned long ago that I can and do make time for what's important for my well-being. Self-care for me is my daily early morning ritual of prayer, reading, and meditation. I treasure and protect this time no matter where I am, because it's a precious opportunity to continue to grow. When time permits, my weekly bike-riding, just being in nature, exercising and weight training, listening to music, breaking bread with friends and family periodically, and yearly silent retreats when I'm called to go away, are all crucial for my life—for my health and spiritual well-being.

I hear many excuses, "I don't have time" or "there's not enough time" or "you don't work, I still do." The last statement used to make me angry, but I have to find humor in it now. I understand no one knows unless you walk in another's shoes, not to take it personally. Our bodies, minds, and hearts will suffer in different ways if we don't make time to nurture our most important friendship, the one I have with Jesus. I ask Him to forgive me when I complain about the endless cycles of my daily life as being wasted and meaningless. I truly do believe He values even the ordinary, but I lose sight of that sometimes. I admit, at times, my life feels quite boring and mundane. When I hear others' stories of exotic trips, pilgrimages, and traveling to extraordinary places, my Lord is quick to bring to mind that my life too, is filled with awe, amazement, miracles and blessings beyond what I can count. It is a God-driven life, and for that I am grateful, no longer feeling useless or boring. Is it perfect and without sin? Hell no! But, I know He loves me just as I am … unconditionally.

When I feel tired, whether physically, emotionally, mentally or spiritually, it's time to rest. It's time to slow down, relax, and surrender, which requires patience on my part. Accept the help He so freely is ready to give to our weary souls. Remember nothing we do in the name of

Jesus is meaningless. Our efforts for the Lord are never in vain. "Let us not become weary in doing good, for at the proper time we will reap a harvest if we do not give up." (Galatians 6:9)

—Denise Broussard

*For your reflection*: When you are feeling tired and weary, will you rest and accept what He offers you?

*The Lord, the God of gods, has spoken and summoned the earth from the rising of the sun to its setting. From Zion, God shines forth, perfect in beauty. Our God comes and will not be silent! —Psalm 50:1-3*

## Ode to a Lily Pad

The continual spiral of hope reaches
intently for inspiration and expression
of what is held deeply in its center.

A million different paths the journey takes,
originating from its core, incentive known
only by the heart.

What source is this that calls the heart to seek,
always searching for an utterance of sense
and beauty validating the energy provoked.

The desire for growth is evergreen,
pushing upward and outward toward the stars,
the element from which it came.

What benevolent source animates this power
from its center? This amazing being that creates
every living thing with such meaning

and particularity, even to its shadow side.
There is beauty and meaning in every
detail, if only the eye sees

in pause and wonder from the
eyes of the heart, beating in
unison with our Creator.

—Velma LeBlanc Cheramie

*For your reflection:* Is God calling forth from your deepest self, something new? Is there something from your shadow side that he is calling you to move away from? Spend time with him and listen. Let him lead you on this journey of change.

*Standing near the cross of Jesus were his mother, his mother's sister, Mary of Clopas, and Mary Magdalene. —John 19:25*

## Standing Beneath the Cross

In my life, I've felt myself carrying the cross of suffering since I was a young girl. The weight, so heavy for long periods of time, but I now know I was never carrying it alone. Storms of life come and go, and I'm happy to say I now find comfort along the way.

To hang on the cross yourself, in your own pain, can feel overwhelming with loneliness. Even Jesus hanging on the cross cried out, "My God, my God, why have you forsaken me?" In spite of what happens, He was not abandoned and neither are we.

I've stood beneath the cross of many loved ones' suffering. Being there for loved ones through long-term illnesses and eventually death. Waiting for test results and watching their bodies deteriorate in front of my eyes. Listening to stories of childhood trauma, unhealed wounds, and living with depression. Witnessing loved ones sink deep into all types of addictions, unable to take their pain away or fix them.

Standing beneath the cross for loved ones can be exhausting. It's why I say and believe I don't stand alone, ever. My help, my strength, my endurance, my determination, my willingness, comes only from my Lord. I don't always get it right but I do the best I can. Without Him, I can do nothing. I now understand that within me is a power greater than myself. It's the only way I can stand beneath the cross with hope, compassion, and love.

—Denise Broussard

***For your reflection:*** Can we stand as Mary did? Standing in strength, refusing to give back in kind, transforming rather than transmitting?

## All In

I step on ancient stones,
Earth and sand compacted over the millennia,
Formed through pressure,
The stones that the ancients trod,
I step in footprints of ancestors.

Spirit draws me
Calls me to follow the path,
A path to places where I sometimes don't want to go.
Spirit says, "Trust where I lead you,
I draw you to the way that leads to me.

There is no happenstance.
You are in this place,
On this path for a reason.
Come with an opened heart,
On this path to wholeness.

Move from the shadows,
Away from comfort,
Away from old ideas and ways,
Away from stagnation,
Away from things that deplete.

Step into light,
Walk the path of faith to trust,
Search out truth.
See with new eyes,
See the openness that lies before you.

Feel the cleansing breeze,
Blowing away complacency,
Clearing out the old ways,
Bringing renewal.
Be refreshed!

Be emboldened,
Follow the path,
Go around the bend,
Discover,
Be all in."

—Trudy Gomez

*For your reflection*: Do you trust enough to be all in?

*The shadow is the greatest teacher for how to come to the light.*
—Ram Dass

## In the Shadows

If I can begin to name you
I would love to call you friend.
Sometimes it is true.

Sometimes, in your friendship
I recognize conduct
that I experience
as unloving or hurtful
yet I am able to
move away from it.
I don't attach.

Ah, but then the time comes
when the intent and the
reflections are so incomprehensible
I can't find the picture and the
story to tie all the pieces
together.

I am caught up in the
Candle-less darkness
unable to uncover the
affiliation of
where does this fit?
Why am I seeing this?
Agony begins.

Why does my reaction
cause distress when
"that" isn't mine?
I'm not "that."

Is "this" or "that"
true in my ego?

And the scrutiny continues,
relentlessly.
Simmering at times,
boiling over at times.
Plumbing the depths,
I search for pieces
of information.

Then, unearthed,
always one truth.
It's not my business
what others do
or say.
Liberation arrives
and I breathe again.

—Avis Lyons Leblanc

*For your reflection*: When you are caught in the agony of "why does
this upset me so?" Or in finding someone else wrong, you might ask
yourself, "Whose business am I trying to manage?"

# Encounter and Enlightenment

Photo by Denise Broussard

*Jesus asked her,"Why are you crying? Who are you looking for?" She thought he was the gardener and said, "Sir, if you have taken his body away, please tell me, so I can go and get him." Then Jesus said to her, "Mary!" She turned and said to him,"Rabboni." The Aramaic word "Rabboni" means "Teacher." —John 20:15–16*

## I Have Seen the Lord

Walking beside Love during the pain
of the crucifixion.
This courage I seek.

She holds space for Love's earthly pilgrimage,
her heart open to his apostles.
This expansion of nothingness
reaches my soul.

Love said, "Mary!"
and her eyes opened to truth.
This freedom I recognize.

Mary of Magdala, willing, thirsting, courageous,
Apostle of the Apostles, in love with Love.
If only to see the Lord as you did
and live my life, transformed.

—Deidre Montgomery

*For your reflection*: Would you know the Lord if He said your name?

*I wrote this poem to accompany a recent watercolor painting. The more I painted, the more I began to remember in great detail this man who was a part of my early childhood. I wish I had known him as an adult, but am satisfied that these memories from my heart are my love letter to him.*

## Buster Washington

Big, rounded toes caked with mud and dirt,
shabby and dirty with the smell of grease and oil.
Boots coming ... boots going. You were everywhere.
As my memory awakens, I recall:
life on a cotton farm wasn't kind to feet or hands.

Your skin was dark—very dark.
"Jane, if you drink black coffee, you gonna turn black."
Smiling, I watched my vanilla wafers floating one at a time in my black
coffee. Spooning them out, I wondered why someone would say that
to me.

Your smile was big and white.
Your knowing eyes were supposed to be white, but they were a dirty yellow.
You were old ... I was six.
You were Buster ... and I was Miss Jane.

Something was odd about you and me.
I was always shy and you were, too—bowing and tipping your hat when
I would pass.
When I spoke, you would reply "Yes, ma'am."
My heart felt comfortable—but also uncomfortable with you.
What did you feel?

You were meek, humble, and joyful, too.
You worked without question.
No task was too great, but life for you was hard.
Daddy was careful in choosing your work.
You moved slowly ... deliberately each and every day ...
your steps seemingly laborious, as you lifted your heavy, ill-fitted boots.

I wonder if the cold and the heat tested your spirit as I peered at you through the windows. In the winter, you ate in the tractor shed. In the summer, you ate under the pecan tree where I made mudpies.

Sometimes, if you were lucky, you enjoyed a home-cooked meal. Most times your meal was the same: two fried Cotto salami sandwiches, mayo, cheese, and tomato on a flimsy paper plate.

Your smiling face, glistening with sweat, always seemed to say,
"Here I am ... and I can still smile even through this struggle."
As I delivered your lunch, there was always a soft "Thank you, Miss Jane." Gently you would take the plate, as you battled the flies for your lunch. Mama would soon call for me to come in to eat. I always felt uncomfortable leaving you alone under that tree.

Life on a farm ...
in the south ... in the 60s ... that's just the way it was.
Deep down, my heart knew "I am not a Miss; I'm just a little girl."
Something wasn't right.
Even then, my heart worked perfectly
as the soul always knows what's right ... and what's wrong.

My words are my tribute to you, Buster.
What I sensed then, but appreciate now,
is that you were a man, pure of spirit with a big heart,
quick to laugh and quicker to smile.
With your twinkling eyes and calloused hands
you truly were all that is meant to be in each of us.

You lived your life in humble acceptance.
Your kind heart seemed to scream through your actions:
"Love and care for each other—no matter what!"
And now, as memories tucked away begin to resurface,
I ask, "Isn't that what we are all here for?"

Your life is a reminder to soften our hearts, to set aside our egos to embrace kindness, compassion, and humility. And, if my faith is correct and you are only a "whisper away," may you realize that your life, one spent on an obscure country cotton farm, left an important footprint on a little girl's life.

—Jane DeBlieux

*For your reflection*: Do you believe that your soul always knows what is right and what is wrong? Try to remember a time in your childhood when your soul spoke to you.

*Be gracious to me, O God, be gracious to me. For my soul takes refuge in you; and in the shadow of your wings I will take refuge until destruction passes by. —Psalm 57:1*

## In the Shadow of God's Wings

It bears repeating that when I take time to just be in His presence, amazing things happen. Graces are given daily, even through distractions. Awareness has been a slow process, but I am seeing with a new set of eyes when I go into silence.

This was the last day of my eight-day silent retreat as I sat in the dining area for a fabulous lunch. I was facing the door that has a top window so I could see outside. I always sit in a different area, different table, with a different vantage point at every meal. I could see the sun shining through the trees. I thought of His light. Not believing my eyes, I could see rain falling at the same time.

My thoughts on rain were washing away sins, worries, concerns, and sadness. I literally jumped up immediately and went outside to walk in the rain, looking for the rainbow. For me rainbows are His promise that I am never alone. Rainbows happened the two previous years while on retreat in this same place. I'm asking, could this blessing be happening for three years in a row?

Some might say this is all coincidence, but I no longer believe in coincidence. I was feeling the sunlight and the rain hitting my face, all the while walking the grounds in anticipation … looking up at the sky to catch a glimpse of a rainbow. No rainbow was ever seen, but what did fall literally at my feet was a large beautiful brown feather. If that's not a promise from Jesus saying "I am with you always," I don't know what is.

I've read that feathers represent freedom, flight, caring from heaven above, moving beyond our set of beliefs and boundaries. Brown feathers signify grounding, relating to enduring it all, and still going strong. They signify home, friendships, and respect. For certain Native American tribes, to receive a feather meant they went up against the enemy and were victorious. This beautiful brown feather, God's wing, loved one's wings who have gone to their final home, all represent my guardian angels. This one brown feather told me loud and clear, I am on the right path in the shadow of God's wings.

—Denise Broussard

*For your reflection:* Do you feel God's covering of protection and loving care?

*If not us, then who? If not now, then when?* —*John Lewis*

## The Light of Eve's Smile

I have just come home from a two-day hospital stay. I had the care of some really exceptional professionals who were "my team." Among those folks was a CNA named Eve. I would guess her to be late twenties or early thirties.

Quiet and efficient, Eve was pleasant but not actually friendly nor did she exhibit much of a sense of humor. Jerry engages with everyone, but she just wouldn't participate.

The first time she came to take my vitals as they say, she completed her job and picked the trash bags out of all four of the cans. I remarked, "Eve, you just do it all." She looked at me like I wasn't fully aware of life as it is lived and she said, "Everyone should. If you see trash needs to be picked up, do it," and she left. I was impressed by her matter-of-fact comment and very impressed with her view of personal responsibility. What an example for me to see. I didn't see many others doing the same. One other, Cassie, was like that.

The next day was a pretty busy day for me, and I didn't see much of Eve. Night-time came and we fell back into routine. She came every two hours for vitals.

I went to sleep around nine and woke up at midnight in a bed that was fully drenched! I jumped up, hit the call button, and started trying to get my gown off all the while pulling my IV pole around and stripping my bed. A nurse rushed in, unplugged me, and said she would send someone to help me because she had an emergency elsewhere.

During this whole flurry of activity Eve came in to take vitals. I'm saying to her how I don't know where anyone is and I need help with my bed. I was probably much more flustered than was called for, but I was quite distressed. At least by this time I had a clean gown on and was loose from my IV pole. I would have remade my bed but I had no clean linens so I just sat in a chair.

Very quietly Eve said, "I will change your bed. I need to get clean linens." When she returned with the linens, she started to put the bed together, I went to the other side to help spread the covers. Eve looked straight at me and smiled. It was a beautiful, quiet, accepting smile; and it was an unexpected gift. She then became very consoling, quietly telling me she would pick up all the dirty linens and then come back to finish her job, not to worry.

Just that little bit of assistance I offered changed her whole demeanor toward me. She doesn't seem like someone who smiles often, but I don't know how she is when not at work. I know that Eve has given me a real example of service and personal dignity.

And she gave me the gift of that gentle smile that I don't think is easily given.

—Avis Lyons LeBlanc

*For your reflection:* Where have you found an unexpected light? And, perhaps, some life lessons?

## Incarnation

See.
Look right into my heart.
I am wrapped in the world,
and the world is in me.
We are so united,
when you gaze for a while
you will see yourself.
We hold all the compassion,
all the suffering
all the joy and
all the laughter of our world.
Peace be with you.

—Betty Landreneau

*For your reflection*: What experiences bring you to an awareness of
your participation in incarnation?

*But when he, the Spirit of truth, our God, comes, he will guide you into all truth. He will not speak on his own; he will speak only what he hears, and he will tell you what is yet to come. —John 16:13*

## A Taste of the Rapids

Life lessons are learned on the rapids of the Colorado and Roaring Fork Rivers. Pushing through fear with God's help and a reminder that He is our guide. Fear, anticipation, and adrenaline are at an all-time high. Everyone on the river is friendly, happy, and ready to help. That shared joy of living helped us let go of our fear.

Driving through Glenwood Canyon, we travel through the narrow gorge. The beauty of the canyon takes your breath away. Sections of this roadway features No-Name Tunnel, Hanging-Lake Tunnel, and Reverse-Curve Tunnel … one of the most expensive highways ever to be built. Along this ride we were hugging the north bank of the Colorado River, while the Union Pacific Railroad occupies the south bank.

Hopping on a 16-foot raft through roughly six miles of the most beautiful scenery, the rapids are many, and the most exciting is the South Canyon. The power of water is unleashed. Blessed with Mr. Bob, an outdoor specialist of 50 years, he immediately makes it clear that he is our guide, and we are now feeling confident. We learn very quickly to listen to his voice. He is constantly shouting, "Row forward, row backwards!" We are at ease, yet so excited, and this brings to mind that God is truly our guide in life … if we'd just listen.

Mr. Bob is so knowledgeable about the Colorado River. He makes us aware of all the different plants and even stops for us to smell the ponderosa pine tree. He says, "Press your nose against the bark, what do you smell?" Amazingly, I smelled butterscotch and vanilla. He points out two American Bald Eagles which he has named. Of course, the female is Independence, and the male, Freedom. Our lives depend on listening to this guide. I'm reminded to slow down and listen to my Guide above.

We also immediately understand how important it is to work together. When he hollers his command, we need to move our oars in rhythm. Our safety depends on it, and our working together makes all the difference in the success of our moving through smaller ripples or intense rapids. When he hollers, "Stop!" We'd better listen. From afar we can see the huge boulders we are about to meet. We listen to our guide reminding us to lock our feet and prepare to lean in. Makes me think of the many life obstacles that threaten us. If only we'd listen to God. He too, whispers in a soft voice, "lean in, listen to me."

As we maneuver our way through the rapids of life, we don't have to do it alone. We have each other. We will go through trials, losses, difficulties, but our Lord says, "Look, I am with you and will watch over you wherever you go." Genesis: 28:15

We turn to Him and to each other when those rocks or boulders get in our way. During our three-hour adventure we came upon a few rapids that weren't so bad, and a few that were downright scary, but we continued to listen to Mr. Bob and work together. After each one, no matter how easy or difficult, he would shout, "High Five!" We had been instructed to raise our oars together in celebration of our accomplishments. Fear had been overcome, and we celebrated our victory. Another reminder of God calling us to celebrate our lives together. "Therefore encourage one another and build each other up, just as in fact you are doing."
1Thessalonians: 5:11

—Denise Broussard

*For your reflection*: Are you listening to your guide to carry you forward, working with each other, then celebrating with your fellow woman or man?

# Gifts and Callings

Photo by Wendi Romero

*Playing with the 5, 7, 5 syllables of Haiku helps me move into silence and be present with the specific.*

**Haiku to Living Life**

Simple earthen pots
beautiful with daily use
hold this great treasure.

Mold, crack, re-mold.
The clay jar of my being
Finds new ways to be.

Happy the mended
until the next fissure comes
care and love repair.

Burnished with intent
that life is worth the risks
remain in the fray.

—Avis Lyons LeBlanc

***For your reflection***: Notice how you support your earthen pot.

*Nothing ever really goes away. It just changes into something else.*
—*Sarah Ockler*

## The Shape of Everything

Notice a shape
before it morphs
into something else.

Everything is always
in the process
of becoming.

Every cloud,
its own destination,
each its own sea.

From lily to pad,
laying flat on
its aging back

wrinkling in the sun,
a holding place for
droplets of dew

on their way
to becoming
something new.

Life presses in
from all sides,
the next shape

already there,
waiting in the soil
of holy darkness.

What dormancy lies
hidden in me?
What shape might I become?

—Wendi Romero

*For your reflection*: What might be waiting to take shape in you?

*Women need friends. Solid friendships that mean a listening ear, a shoulder to lean on, to be understood by another, and not demanding of each other, to remind each other that we are not alone. Faith meeting faith.*

## Love and Sacrifice

Jesus endured indescribable pain, to the point of bringing me to tears when I think of what He did for all of us. His love and sacrifice are amazing graces which bring to mind my dear friend, Cynthia.

In 2017, I was sitting at the Kitchenary Shop thinking of Jesus and my long-time friend of over forty years. My sister-in-Christ, Cynthia and I, had attended our last retreat together in 2013. When the Jesuit Spirituality Center in Grand Coteau, La. reopened after renovations, I registered the two of us for a retreat. She had just been diagnosed on 12/12/12 with acute lymphoblastic leukemia, "ALL", along with the Philadelphia Chromosome, an abnormality of chromosome 22. The diagnosis was shocking and scary, but I believed she would make the retreat, if God was willing.

Silent retreats for me began in 1998 when I called Cynthia and asked her if she would attend one with me. I was curious, or so I thought. She agreed, so I checked into the Jesuit Spirituality Center's yearly calendar and now believe that God led me to this retreat, "Looking at your Life" with Paula D'Arcy. I asked Cynthia if she had ever heard of her and she had not. Little did I know at the time, what I thought to be pure curiosity, our Lord had a whole other agenda. Our first retreat with Paula D'Arcy was in September 1998, and we attended annual retreats with her for the next twenty-two years. Paula's very first talk in the chapel was her story of how she became a pregnant widow at the young age of twenty-seven. A few months after losing her husband and young daughter in a drunk-driving accident, Paula, the sole survivor of that accident, gave birth to another daughter which she raised alone. Cynthia and I immediately looked at each other because this is my story, too. Different circumstances, but both widows at the same age with a precious daughter to raise while overcoming tremendous grief. This silent retreat became another avenue of my spiritual journey which continues to this day.

We were together again in November 2013, with Paula leading a retreat entitled,"A Path and a Small Light." It would be Paula's first retreat back at the Jesuit Spirituality Center in a couple of years. We were so blessed, and it felt like a reunion of sisters once more, but this would be the last time Cynthia and I would attend a retreat on these holy grounds together.

Cynthia suffered off and on for four years, just as Jesus did, with much love, faith, and courage. There are so many words to describe her: wife, mother, daughter, sister, friend, loving, giving, strong, fighter, compassionate, a great listener, funny, prayer warrior, and more. She was so faithful to her Lord and continued to encourage us by her example. She was an inspiration to so many, giving all who loved her the time they needed to let her go.

In spite of our tears, sadness, and even some anger, there is an indescribable peace that I have within. I know without a doubt, that she is brand-new … no more pain, no more suffering. We can no longer share her smiles, laughter, and hugs, but I know when she left this earth, our Lord reached out his hand and said, "Hallelujah, you're home!" Now, I have my friend for a guardian angel.

Yes, we are all here on this planet, some for longer than others. While Cynthia was here, her family and friends were blessed with her love and dedication, along with her contribution to other people's happiness in so many ways. She found the true meaning of life and certainly made a difference in mine. Love and sacrifice, amazing grace … her gift to so many.

—Denise Broussard

*For your reflection*: Think about a friend who had a huge impact on your life and let them know how much they mean to you.

*We can't judge the lives of others because each person knows only their pain. It's one thing to feel you're on the right path, but it's another to think that yours is the only path.* —*Paulo Coehlo*

## The Artist

I don't recall his name
but I watched him
doodle on
an empty page.

He drew diamonds,
overlapping squares and
diagonals, adding depth
to his dimensions.

A famous poet
had arrived in town
and I sat on edge just
to take in her words.

The artist had wandered
into the wrong room,
totally unaware of who
the teacher was.

Then his phone rang,
and while the poet
was reciting her poem,
he answered the call.

The hair on my neck
stood at attention.
How obnoxious, I thought.
He doesn't even care.

Such distraction and now
everyone's focus is cut in two.
Before we begin to write our
own poems, he asked for a break.

Then the lesson comes—
"write what you've noticed,
what you've lost, and
what you've found."

Like a razor meeting skin,
the artist zoomed in.
Like a burning laser,
he cut through.

Words replaced his shapes
on the page and
when he was done
he apologetically spoke.

It was his ailing mother
on the phone and
he's the only lifeline
she's ever known.

I realized then
that it wasn't about
squares or diamonds,
but the angle of his life.

He was living the depths
of the diagonal
as best he could,
the only way he knew how.

—Wendi Romero

*For your reflection:* We travel each our own paths on this journey
through life. No two paths are ever the same, so be cautious when you
feel a tendency to judge.

*The King will answer them, truly I tell you, just as you did it to one of the least of these who are members of my family, you did it to me. —Matthew 25:40. For even the Son of Man did not come to be served, but to serve. —Mark 10:45*

## My Calling

Living, loving, serving,
all worth diving into.
Questions asked
all my life.
Answers right there
in front of me.

Acceptance sometimes
takes a lifetime.
Accepting that where I am
at any given moment
is where God
has called me to be.

Accepting when
God calls me to silence.
I don't question,
I just say yes.

Encouraging others
through their trials.
Being peace in chaos.
Embracing it.

Caring for the sick,
striving to do good for others
in their time of need.
Owning it.

Living with a grateful heart,
praying continually.
Always giving thanks
no matter the circumstance.
Holding it.

It's time to accept that
I am defined
by my faithfulness
to do whatever God
has placed in front of me.

That is my success.
I'm finally embracing,
owning, holding, and accepting
my unique calling,
giving up the search.

—Denise Broussard

*For your reflection*: Whenever we meet the needs of others, we answer God's call. Are you struggling with your call to serve?

*My walks in nature invite the wonder of found treasures no longer dynamic:*
*life is past. I see such treasures and I want to give them life again.*

## My Basket of Gifts

Shells collected on the beach.
Rocks and dried plants
from rivers and mountains.
Artifacts from deserts.
All beckon,
"Come to the spirit of this place."

These touchstones connect me
to the magnificence
of ourselves as nature,
and the splendid peace
of being part of the creation story.

I am a gatherer.
A noticer of fragments.
A saver of lovelies.
These skeletons
of what was once alive and vibrant
now reminders of nature as it is.

The elements you will find
on my altars
are found gifts
from wandering
the paths of forests
and river beds.
Oceans and deserts.
Mountains and valleys.

Treasures gathered
to place on my altars,
honoring life
in all its phases.

—Avis Lyons Leblanc

*For your reflection:* How might you create an altar that expresses your celebration of life?

# Grieving and Growing

Photo by Trudy Gomez

*In the process of letting go, you will lose many things from the past, but you will find yourself. —Deepak Chopra*

**Door Prize at Round Top Poetry Festival**

I learned many things that early spring day. I learned that the deceased poet, John Ashbery, was a fan of collage. His metaphors sliced and stuck just like the sharp edges of the small pictures and words he used to cut and paste. We sat in a chapel memorializing dead poets, reading their poems aloud, and bringing each of their legacies back to life. Following each tribute, a door prize was given in honor of the deceased poet. Just as a woman on the stage held up sharp blue scissors and Elmer's glue, I heard my named called. With amusement, I stood up to receive my prize.

When I was six years old, I got my very first pair of orange rounded scissors. I cut everything in sight—the Sears catalog, frayed margins of paper, postcards from places I'd never been, my parents' wedding picture. They seemed so happy that day, the day they said "I do" to each other. The next year, it got bitterly cold and I contracted pneumonia. Their frozen smiles in the photo thawed with every hardship they faced. In the old shoebox my mother kept, I searched through the black and white images, but couldn't seem to find much evidence of happier times.

My father died before his hair turned gray and my mother never let me forget "the cutting" of his right hand in the picture as he was about to feed her a piece of wedding cake. She just couldn't let it go. So, forty years later I searched for the paper pieces of her shattered past, trying to make sense of slices in time. I glued the tattered ends of my parents' beginning back together again, and took it to a place specializing in restoration of old damaged photos. In three days, an 8 x 10 glossy finish resurrected the innocence of their special day, an innocence that had diminished over time by some cruel turns and the unexpected wounds of life.

That day in a photograph, before things fell apart and yellowed with time, was pieced back together, in a single act. In the old image, now made new, other images began to emerge. I saw my bright-eyed teen-aged mother in her white-tiered wedding dress, and my handsome olive-skinned father in his sharp suit … young unweathered faces with eyes fixed on just each other. They held so much hope for a long life together. This day, I watched my mother as she stood speechless, staring at a moment in time upon which all her other subsequent moments were built. The deep lines in her face softened and a tear escaped the corner of her eye. She gazed at the reflection of their young love made visible again, now joined together like a renewed vow. She held the picture as steady as she could while her glacier of bitterness began to melt. Love, long hidden from sight, now brought back to life in her small trembling hands.

—Wendi Romero

*For your reflection:* What do you need to let go of today?

## I Dreamed of You Last Night

I dreamed you were lying in our bed next to me.
I felt your breath and the heat of your body.
I murmured, "Oh, you are here."
The heat of your body drew me.
I snuggled next to you,
I lay my head on your chest.
It all felt so real,
Then I realized you were not physically there.
Thank you for the comfort,
For letting me know you are here with me.

—Trudy Gomez

*For your reflection:* They are never gone. We will always be.

*A few years ago, I learned that a family member had passed away, someone I should have known on a personal level. Learning the news conjured up feelings of loss and regret.*

## Alicia

My cousin, Alicia, died last night.
I knew her
but I didn't.

Being older, she was
not around much
when I was growing up.
She seemed to have
had a full life … or so I hope.
I knew her
but I didn't.

My why is justified
by our age difference
but now falls flat on my heart.

My footprints and her footprints
began in the same place.
So where were we
all these years?
Sometimes family
are the most foreign to us all.

This feeling, a different one
was for me, a wondering,
a curiosity
of a life so close
but yet so far.

Flipping to another station, I see
the east coast on the morning news:

another blizzard, snow-piled streets,
footprints in the snow, slowing disappearing
as the world turns white
and goes on.

Alicia …
her life, her footprints
made an impression and moved forward
one step at a time, and then,
a gradual fade …
pulled from this world
into the next,
to walk some more.

Alicia died last night.
I knew her
but I didn't.

—Jane DeBlieux

*For your reflection:* Are there people in your own family that you need
to connect with? Don't wait to learn about them through their eulogy.

*Denial helps us to pace our feelings of grief. It is nature's way of letting in only as much as we can handle. —Elizabeth Kübler-Ross and David Kessler*

**Goodbye Is for Never**

I said goodbye to my son when he went away to college. I said goodbye again when he died. Did I say goodbye? I know I didn't. I know I continued to hold that he was out there in life doing his living. The only thing is, he hasn't aged. He is still 31 years old with a youthful smile and happy eyes. His hair a little long for the times and he is still tall, big, and happy. He made happiness a choice and looked for joy in his life. I know all was not happiness with him, just like for everyone, but he chose to be happy. He was active in his Church and with his children, coaching Justin's baseball team. He belonged to a club for black powder hunting, and was an avid hunter and fisherman. Mike took in life and did what a good man does.

I just let myself believe that my weekly call was coming. I haven't gotten a phone call.

I do get little glimpses of love and sweetness he sends me. He touches in from time to time, and I say hello when he pops into my head. I know he is well.

We had a conversation the day of his funeral. I was in the bathroom putting on my make-up and I heard him say, "Mamma." I knew he was with me. He told me that he and his wife, Elayne, had decided that if something happened to them both, that "We want Daddy to raise the children."

I said, "Why, Mike? You know Jerry and I would love them and care for them much better than Alton."

"I know, Mamma. "He said, "But Daddy is more 'like us.'"
I took that to mean the hunting, fishing, and camping stuff. I'm not sure what he meant. Did I ask? Did he say?

I wish I could remember the rest of our conversation; he was his usual soft-spoken, sweet self. I am sure it ended with "I love you," as our conversations always did. I wasn't even surprised that he came to visit; it was so very natural, as if he was in the room.

I stayed for over a week to help Elayne navigate the "what now" things, and on one of our errands she told me that she and Mike had decided that if something happened to them both, Alton was to raise the children. She also told me that she had decided absolutely not! Alton had been Alton at the funeral and she didn't want him to have the children. They would come to me and Jerry.

The children did spend their summers with us until they became adults and went into the work world.

I am recently, this new year of 2020, experiencing a new place in this grief process. He died in 1993. I am finding I did have some places in my heart that needed some healing, and I have offered them attention. It had to do with forgiving myself for not being the best mother in his young years, and forgiving myself for not being a better advocate for him with his father as he was a developing young person. That may not be all, but it is what it is for now. Time will show me.

Saying goodbye to your child when he dies is not something a mother expects to do. It isn't the natural progression of life. I didn't say goodbye, or maybe what I mean is, I don't think I grieved the way people say grief is supposed to be. I don't know, and it's been a long time. I also know goodbye is for never when your child is in your heart, so much of your life is wrapped up in that special relationship. They can never be gone. The love is too big for gone.

—Avis Lyons LeBlanc

*For your reflection*: Has grief been different for you than it's "supposed" to be?

## Grief

Grief—its monosyllabic power overrides any and every
moment, molecule, mountain, river, task. A snowfall of loss

becomes a spear of penetration to the marrow of my soul.
Oddly, while grief waves its own scavenger wings over my

very beingness, swallowing me whole, I know I'm fully alive.
My body descends like a fledgling, free-falling from a once

warm nest, a fabric woven of twigs, thorns, leaves, and memories
puncture my body that has begun to ache and writhe

with a pain so electric, exhausting, exacting that I don't want to live
anymore. There is a salt of sorrow that shatters the prisms of

peace and no matter how hard I try, I cannot find a way to die.
The uncertain field of change is now in charge, right where love

was once as easy to express as cracking an egg. The heft and
circumstance of empty becomes the new companion.

I wish we could be friends, grief and I, he visits so frequently now.

—Sidney Creaghan

*For your reflection:* Is there a particular grief that needs more of your
attention? If so, get your colors and let your hands choose the colors at
random to fill the paper. Then, after looking at the coloring for a while,
take a few deep breaths and ask it, the image, if it has anything to say to
you, and does it have a title? It will tell you. Write them on the page or
the other side. Put the date on it.

## Missing Pieces

When your heart is broken, shattered,
And your life no longer resembles what it once was
How do you gather the missing pieces and put them back together again?

How do you go on when your life no longer resembles
what it once was when there are pieces missing?
How can a heart's missing pieces be so heavy,
like a black hole in space—
The pull of it so strong
Drawing all matter and mass into darkness,
Making it so dense that light doesn't escape?

Though my heart is ravaged by grief
I turn to You in my pain.
You absorb it, You absorb me
You sooth the ache.

When the storm rages within,
I stop and turn my eyes to You, the Calm.
In that moment, peace fills those broken places

And all is well.

—Trudy Gomez

*For your reflection:* Grief has no time limit, no boundaries.

## To Grieve

I imagine each of us must know grief by this time in our lives. Some of us are more familiar with it than others. Grief is overwhelming. Grief is in a class by itself. It is all-encompassing and stops the daily routine, and the usual comings and goings in life. It is an extraordinary time.

To grieve comes from the Latin word, *gravis,* meaning grave, heavy; *gravare,* to burden. It is a time of anguish, lament, distress, and loss of hope. We mourn, cry, and distress. We are in the full throttle of bereavement. It is a lonely time, and loneliness will bring its double-edged self, a palpable ache, with it. At least it does for me.

Yet, one of its most dramatic characteristics is memory. We spend hours, days, months, and years remembering the loved one we have lost. I find that when in grief, I live more in memory than in the real world. Life is in the real world. But grief is a time of not being in the present moment. We look at old photographs, reread letters from our lost one, talk about our lost one with family and friends. We reminisce. Forty years ago seems like yesterday and yesterday feels like forty years ago. We hear the bell toll.

Our whole life is changed through grief. It continues to change as the hours, days, weeks, years, and the lamenting go by. It is a time of immense passage within our self. Death and grief, like birth and aging, are part of our life cycle. Part of the natural flow from the moment we are born.

—Sidney Creaghan

*For your reflection:* The only thing permanent is change. You might reflect on an area in your life you'd like to change before you die.

# Healing and Hoping

Photo by Wendi Romero

## Great Acadiana Flood of August 2016

Listening to the primordial song of wind and thunder and rain
Twelve, twenty-four, forty-eight hours
Sometimes a pause, a drip, then the steady beat of torrents
Seemingly never-ending water falling from a dark, menacing sky
A horrible beauty.

Water rising and rising
Streaming through ditches, coulees, bayous, and rivers,
Overfilling, overflowing banks and levees
Still the rain falls and water rises
Water seeking least resistance
Each cloud burst releasing mighty, awful awesome torrents.

Watching …
with wonder and trepidation.
At times, stepping out from sheltered space
gauging the steady rise
seeing once-green pastures and dry lawns
first pools, then ponds, then lakes from a steady rise of the river
Watching the sky still dark with clouds,
ladened,
burdened.
Looking for a break, a clearing
nothing but shades of gray and silver fills the vision.

Morning …
No sound of thunder.
No flash of lighting.
No sound of rain
Stepping out of shelter, surveying nature's handiwork.
A brightening sky.
Water where none should be,
inundated homes
up to rafters
over roofs.

Birds venturing out from their sheltered space of tree,
bush, and shrubs,
rabbits nibbling in garden beds,
spiders repairing webs,
doves on a power line,
all offering hope in the face of helplessness;
reminders of the powerlessness of man and woman and beast,
the only thing to cling to is Mercy and Love and Saving Grace.

—Trudy Gomez

*For your reflection*: What is your ground in trouble times? Do you come
from a place of hope?

**Lives on Lawns**
(the aftermath of the flood of 2016)

Skeleton walls, everything exposed
Boxes filled with memories and water
Smell of wet damp mixed with bleach
Tears and laughter verging on hysteria
Hold tight, hold tight
Come together, come to center

Fear and relief swirling, dizzying
Adrenalin let down
A shaking that can't be controlled
Trying to come to center
Hold tight, hold tight
Come together in the chaos

Water receded but with
Each new dark cloud
Each new rumble of thunder and flash of lightening
Each rain drop
Anxiety builds.
Will it rise again?
Where is center?
Hold tight, hold tight
Come together

Surveying piles of detritus and debris
Precious possessions and memories on lawns
Piled high house after house
Street after street.
Exposed to passersby, curiosity seekers, strangers
Who whisper to themselves,
Hold tight, hold tight
Come together in the chaos
Hold tight, hold tight ....

—Trudy Gomez

*For your reflection:* What helps you to hold your center in times of anxiety?

*Focus all of your energy not on fighting the old, but on building the new.*
*—Socrates*

## After the Storm

After these days
of rain and ruin,
heaving and havoc,
the sun peeks
through what's left
of the trees.

The rain is over
but I've grown weary.
A pair of sneakers,
old photographs,
and broken glass
just floated by—

wrecking water
in search of a place to go.
Highways and homes
uprooted while
stagnant lakes mirror
mounds of debris.

After these days
of deluge, now calm,
the egrets fly again
and the heron lifts
her wet gray body from
the ravaging waters;

spreading her wings,
gracefully soaring over

what used to be her life.
She will make a new
home for herself.
She always does.

—Wendi Romero

*For your reflection:* Build upon something new.

*We shape clay into the pot, but it is the emptiness inside that holds.*
*—Lao Tzu*

## Handle With Care

For twenty years, a tall slender terracotta jug has graced my patio, and like me she has aged, too. Her curves are still smooth and her edges rounded, but her finish is growing dull and green from weather and wear. One of her handles broke last year and now she has a large chip in her lip, but I'm not ready to throw her out just yet.

Last week I moved her from the dark corner where she spent the winter out into the bright light. I laid her on the ground over soft shoots of grass, her beauty and brokenness simultaneously exposed. I watched the interplay of shadows dance upon her, the sun's rays filling in her flaws. Sue Bender, in her book, *Everyday Sacred,* says that "our imperfections really are our gifts." Places in me where I still fall short came to mind: my impatience at times, my compulsivity and perfectionism, my need to fix, and my inability to sometimes let things be what they simply are. I recalled how she, too, was formed from the primary elements of earth, water, air, and fire; then turned, held, and shaped in the hands of the Potter.

I see her as a sacramental piece, a sacred statue, representative of a far deeper reality. Before her glaze hardened with heat, lines like an artist's signature had been pressed into her. In pondering her contour from all angles, I encountered my own image. She emerged from the kiln, precious and whole, but everything about her appearance said "please handle with care." Some of my own edges have been worn smooth, cured and strong, while at my broken places, my surface may still be a bit jagged and sharp.

In her emptiness, she possessed an undeniable strength. She is a mirror, and I see that which I am in the presence of, are one in the same. We are both containers of life. She now holds a thriving ivy given to my family at my father's funeral twenty-eight years ago—a reminder that life continues after death, deep grief is transformative, and beauty can still be found if we seek it.

The hollow of all things, feminine, carries the possibility of always giving birth to something new. We are a meeting place of nature and spirit; an open vessel to be filled, emptied, and filled again. Waters of healing are always flowing, protecting the new life waiting to be formed in us—our own incarnation.

In the words of M.C. Richards, "it wasn't just a jug that I was contemplating, it was my own self."

—Wendi Romero

*For your reflection*: What new life might be waiting to be formed in you?

*Tree of life. All of us, small and large, old and young. We are branches of*
*your one eternal life. Intimately united, unmistakably connected.*
*—Joyce Rupp*


## Anchored in Hope

It's a time of uncertainty.
The threat of a global virus
cannot be denied by the world.
To deny would be unrealistic.
We need stability, strength,
survival, protection.
Just like the mighty live oak tree,
anchored in our Creator's earth.

The trees stand tall and strong
with deep roots.
"When the root is deep,
there is no reason to fear the wind."
No need to panic. No need to carry anxiety.
This too shall pass.

Growing slowly at its own pace,
I've read the oak symbolizes
wisdom, knowledge, and independence.
Growing is a slow process.
Like now, no need to hurry or rush.
With all the shutdowns in place,
we slow down to pray and grow.

The trees invite sunshine
as I invite God's light.
God is light, giving us all
our precious lives on sacred Earth.
We know God's light
did not cause this threat.
He is with us in it and through it.

The mighty oak embraces darkness,
for it is the only way to see stars.
Looking up and recite,
"Star light, star bright,
the first star I see tonight.
I wish I may, I wish I might
have the wish I wish tonight."

Having to go through dark times,
take no one or no thing for granted
in order to see beauty in life.
Enjoy twinkling stars reciting prayers.
Light is there for all in this pandemic.

Trees like us have weathered many storms.
Struck down, but not destroyed.
Broken, but not in despair.
Persecuted, but not abandoned.
The message is clear …
when this virus threatens your life,
be ready to adapt and bend to survive.

The trees and all God's children know
in their souls that they are God's creation.
All people affected by this virus
are embraced by His care, His protection.
Let us not fear.

They know they are loved
by God unconditionally.
He calls us His beloved.
Because of this knowing
we not only have survived,
we can thrive.
Let us have peace.

We are so grateful.
God gently whispers in the breeze,

"Be courageous, stand tall
just like the mighty oak trees.
We are all in this together,
anchored in hope."

—Denise Broussard

*First two quotes by unknown authors

***For your reflection:*** It takes courage to grow and become who you really are. What we need has been within us all along. Can you accept the many ways you are connected to the tree of life? Anchor yourselves in His hope, and no longer fear. Can we recognize during this time of the COVID-19 pandemic, God's presence in kindness, offerings, reaching out in different ways, longer moments of silence, and blessings within the suffering?

*Difficult roads often lead to beautiful destinations. —Zig Ziglar*

**Where Would I Be?**

Born into this world, a baby girl.
Deep feelings of abandonment
I didn't know for years.
God revealed to me later in life
those feelings were there
since in my mother's womb.

A little girl, trusting of others.
Believing in her innocent mind,
no one would do her harm.
Trust shattered by more than one
at a very young age.
Too scared to tell anyone,
knowing no one would believe her.

Those teenage years,
making choices that did not serve her.
Hurting the ones who loved her.
On a road of self-destruction,
spiraling out of control.
I say "her" because I am
no longer that same person.

Where would I be?
If it hadn't been for God
allowing it all to happen.
Giving me time.
Letting me grow.
Letting it be.

My twenties came to reality.
Experiencing the loss
of many loved ones.

Grief and sadness
overwhelmed me.

Where would I be?
If it weren't for God pulling me
out of the pit of despair,
standing my feet on solid ground.

Where would I be?
If it weren't for God whispering
with His still small voice,
"You can trust me. I will never leave you.
I will always love you."

What if God would have abandoned me
as my earthly father did.
In silence, our Heavenly Father
let me know loud and clear …
I was to forgive my father.
What matters is God always loved me,
even before I was born.

The journey to 65 years old
has been a miracle in itself.
Real and colorful.
Full of beauty, trauma, darkness,
light, joy, grief, life, death.

These opposites are held together.
I've needed it all for my health—
just as much as my life depends on
breathing in and breathing out.

I finally accepted my reality.
The endless falling and rising,
allowing feelings and thoughts
to whisper to my heart,
only when I was ready.

Writing ... a way of
explaining to myself
things I do not understand.
I finally start living in mystery.

No longer do I feel the need
to ask that question,
"Where would I be?"
I now trust I have always been
and always will be held
by my Heavenly Father
who will never let me go.

—Denise Broussard

***For your reflection***: Healing is possible. We just need to shift the way we look at our story. Are you ready to accept that you are loved more than you could ever imagine?

*The way of paradox is the way of truth. —Oscar Wilde*

## To Open a Heart

After a month of confinement at home during the COVID-19 pandemic, I realized I was facing an enormous paradox that my wounded heart must learn to navigate.

I had had emergency open-heart surgery during the early days of the virus. As weeks passed, I came to think "open-heart" may have been as much metaphor as literal.

The surgery had made me utterly dependent on other people for a time. I could do nothing on my own: get in or out of bed, walk, sit, bathe, or reach my own hair to comb it. Multiple times a day, other people—of all sizes, all races, all genders, all ages—had their hands on my body while I had no real choice but to surrender to it all.

At the same time, my opened heart had experienced profound connections to some of these people. I learned about the college ambitions of the young woman who cleaned the floor of my room. I heard and shared the profound grief of the ICU nurse on the night shift who had lost her son to a car accident. I was deeply moved by the late-night prayer offered to me by the French-speaking nursing assistant from Côte d'Ivoire.

Then, abruptly, I was home. My recovery was on schedule when, less than a month after I left the hospital, the pandemic arrived. Like everyone else, I was ordered to stay home, to isolate. Seemingly overnight, people became proxy pathogens, dangerous to be near, deadly in fact, something not to touch or be touched by.

Friends could no longer come to help me. I was grateful to be mostly self-sufficient by then. Still, all my valued relationships, activities, and pleasures either disappeared entirely or were converted into sterile electronic forms: emails, texts, phone calls, online gatherings with poorly lit, distorted facial images of people I knew.

The emptiness of sudden and unexpected isolation threatened to overwhelm me. I had finally recognized the profound truth that in order to survive and thrive, I truly needed the support of others. Now, that realization had led me straight to a giant paradox. What I most needed had also become what I most needed to avoid. God had provided a serious spiritual challenge.

As I write this, the pandemic is still in full force around me, still infecting and killing. I remain isolated and am doing the only thing I can do with the paradox. I hold both sides to be true, equally and simultaneously. I absolutely need those whom I need, and my life depends on avoiding them.

However, I also believe God would have it no other way. I suspect the learning that will come from holding these paradoxical, conflicting truths—without abandoning either—is in fact the very path on which my opened heart can fully complete its healing.

—Patricia Drury Sidman

*For your reflection:* What conflicting values or paradoxes are in your life today, and how do you face them?

# Graces and Trials

Photo by Trudy Gomez

*The moment you're about to quit is the moment right before the miracle happens. —Anonymous*

## Rising Waters

It wasn't forecasted and there was no way of knowing that eighteen inches of rain would fall before sunrise the next day. The sound of raindrops on the tin roof had been the sweet lullaby that sang me deeply to sleep. Hours later, in the wee dark hours, I was startled by what I thought to be an intruder shining a bright flashlight in my groggy face. "Surely, this is a nightmare," I thought, but the rush of water into my bedroom instantly and shockingly awakened me.

Water was rising and the search was on for live bodies to get out quickly and move to higher ground. "No time to pack. Just get out NOW, as fast as you can with only the clothes on your back," shouted the rescuer. I sat up in bed and saw waves breaking on my bedroom floor. Another moment of truth rang deep in my bones when I stepped into the cold water, now rising above my knees. I watched my roommate's white tennis shoes float on by. Pictures, loosed from photo albums, candy wrappers, day-old test papers, a Self magazine … all seeking dry ground. With all my possessions submerged, I had no choice but to leave them all behind. Roads were impassable, no cell phones, nor rescue boats to be found. So, I did the only thing I knew to do— to walk to higher ground.

In the dark, I waded from my low-lying street, at times, waist-deep. The only thing I knew for sure, was the direction of the hill and the only friend left in town. By the moonlight I found my way. I was no stranger to floods, but this one I had to rise above all alone. I dug deep just to keep my life afloat. I was twenty years old and had come so far, and I wasn't about to give up now. It was both hell and high water, but I trudged on and by the break of dawn, heaven was the sight of my friend's dry doorstep.

Three days later, in the wake of the flood, attempting to salvage what I could from my life before, I returned to the awful stench left by saturated shag carpet and growing mold. I was especially in search of a test paper, now mealy and smeared with ink. It had been the hardest final exam of my life— the one grade that my professor forgot to record. In class, when he asked for our graded papers to be returned, I came unglued. Like a toddler getting its first shot, I exhaled a loud guttural cry, one I couldn't control. It was the end of a long, challenging semester, and he was asking me for something that I, alone, could not produce.

I attempted to explain and told him of my grade, but he wasn't buying it. I begged him to just give me a lower grade, but please not an "I" for *Incomplete*. My life was now incomplete, and I couldn't bear the thought of repeating this final exam, or worse, having to take his class again. Waterlogged and exhausted, I feared I might just cave and sink.

My dreams were shattered, and that's the day I almost quit college. I couldn't stomach the details and was doubled over in despair. I was consumed by the simple necessities like a dry, safe place to land and a breath of fresh air. I needed time to find my footing … to find myself again. I dropped to my knees and prayed, "Please God, I am face down and I could use a miracle right about now. Give me courage, give me strength, and please, *no more tests*. Please, no more tests for now."

—Wendi Romero

*For your reflection*: Recall a time of utter despair, how you got through it, and how you found yourself again.

## In This Place

I feel as if I am in a place of desolation.
My mind scurries to and fro.
I am scattered
I feel numb
I stand outside of myself
I am in survival mode in my grief.

I long to be gathered,
to find my center.
Then a voice whispers
"Keep your eyes on Me, my sister."
Eat of Me
Taste Me
Consume Me
Be consumed by Me."

Sunday worship seems empty.
I am empty.
The corporal brings no peace, no comfort.
I pray:
"Lord, make me vulnerable to you,
Open my heart,
Companion me!"

Then the music plays,
I sing.
I consume the communion host,
the Body of Christ, my beloved.
I am filled.
I come alive
In this moment,
In this time,
In this place.

—Trudy Gomez

*For your reflection:*
Pray:
Oh my Beloved, come be with me.
Melt my heart.
Oh Holy Fire,
Burn away the loneliness,
Reignite my being.

## On Helping and Being Helped

I still remember a foggy California morning years ago. I was driving to work, when suddenly my car stalled in the left-hand turn lane of a busy highway. Everything had seemed fine when I first signaled my turn and entered the lane. Then my car simply stopped and refused to even try to restart.

I had plenty of gas. I had been driving for a while so I knew the battery had a charge. That was the extent of my ability to diagnose the problem. Meanwhile, cars zipped past me at about 50 mph in both directions while other cars lined up behind me, their drivers growing impatient.

As my anxiety was becoming full-on panic, a car facing me pulled up nose-to-nose with my car. A middle-aged man got out, came to my car, and asked me to open the hood. He reached into the engine of my car and poked around for roughly a minute. Then he asked me to try to start the engine. It turned right over and began sounding normal. He muttered something about "vapor lock" and showed me the little flap he had jiggled.

I was, of course, immensely grateful and thanked him repeatedly. I thought that God must have been looking out for me by sending someone to get me out of that dangerous situation. But then the man said something that changed my perspective forever.

He thanked ME! He told me his wife had left him just that morning; and he was in despair, feeling useless, helpless, in the face of such a loss. He was grateful to have been given an opportunity to feel competent and useful, if only for a minute.

He and I went our separate ways as I realized we can never know for sure who is the helper and who is being helped. When God sends help, even seemingly in response to *our* prayer, He may be sending us to *be* that help for another. All we, I, need do is welcome His presence and offer our willingness.

—Patricia Drury Sidman

*For your reflection:* Are you open to being God's instrument, even when you don't understand what He is doing?

*On the morning of May 21, 2020, I was awakened at 4:20 a.m. Unable to go back to sleep, I got up, made coffee, and sat down in my usual spot to pray. I was prompted to write about the pain and brokenness in my life at the time. This is what poured out as the Spirit revealed those broken areas in my life.*

## The Broken Shell

And so the fake life that was born in me early on was to look good on the outside — shine to all the world. I told myself, "I can do this, right? I have done it for my entire life." Soon my strong defenses would be tested as never before.

I have learned well to stuff the hurt, stuff my feelings, stuff my soul, deep into that little place that no one sees; to cover it up completely. Now, I slowly died. The world was chipping away little pieces of me, day after day after day, until there was nothing left but an empty shell. It washed up on the shore, broken, cracked, abandoned, and lacking all beauty. My facade had washed away with the tide.

As just a shell, I stayed abandoned there for quite some time, and even began to sink deeper and deeper into the abyss of the sand. Tucked away with pain and jagged edges as people walked on by, burying my shell deeper and deeper until I no longer existed.

Then one day from somewhere deep within me appeared my true self. She burst forth and she began digging, shovel in hand and with determination. Her main goal was to dig her shadow self out of that dark, cold sand. As she dug, every person that has betrayed me began to surface, and be let go, as my true self scooped, shoved, and gathered mounds of sand—all the while getting closer and closer to the broken jagged shell.

Reader, perhaps you understand that I was always looking for the beautiful, sparkly new shell of who I thought I *should* be. I polished that shell to a shine of fakeness. It looked good on the outside, but the inside told a very different story. Now, the digging has found my broken shell, and to my surprise, I discovered that, for years, it had been buried in the sand and walked on. Being brought to the surface, then washed away over and over and over again—had done the work of suffering. Now the jagged edges had been polished and the shell brought to a beautiful luster. Now it was my true reflection on the surface of the sand that sparkled and shone so brightly!

Up from the cave of my despair, I realized that in being broken, jagged, and buried deep, I had encountered the love of God the Father, bringing about healing and transformation; moving me to a place of love, joy, and peace. I will never look at a broken shell the same way again. And I can no longer look at my brokenness as a curse—but as a gift that has gotten me to where I am today and that is truly BEAUTIFUL! I can only bless my journey.

—Janice Richard

*For your reflection:* What in you is broken and needs healing?

## The Swift River of Farewell

Even as hearts continue to be
broken open and alone,

it lets us know life is at churn
being lived right where I am

and a toll must often be paid;
the price might be high.

If we are alive this will happen
over and over again.

Each time after the suffering
washes through the swift

river of farewell something unpredictable
has a chance to get redeemed.

But the redemption may take longer
than imagined.

—Sidney Creaghan

*For your reflection*: The word *suffer* comes from the Latin word,
*sufferer: sub,* "from below," and *ferre*, "to bear." I have found that when
a suffering is over, or is moving toward a transition; something new,
a change of some sort, always comes. It usually brings a relief from
the suffering and most always brings us to a new meaning in our life.
Reflect on one of your sufferings by writing about it and see what will
arrive for your well-being or perceptions.

## Yielding

Many are the times that I would have my way,
commanding outcomes to fit my will!
I am lost in confinements of the struggle;
disappointment looms when things go astray.

The current of the Universe is at my hands,
yet I cannot bend it to my will.
I yield to the power of creation, and
in yielding, the power becomes mine.

Invited to join in creation,
I allow the current to sustain me.
I listen for the whisper within me.
My source and being are one.

I yield to you, oh Lord, and in my yielding,
you become my source of power,
all for the greatest good of creation,
finding a rightness within me.

—B. D. Lowry

*For your reflection*: I yield to you, oh God, and move with the Holy
Spirit.

# Learning and Wisdom

Photo by Denise Broussard

*Pursue some path, however narrow and crooked, in which you can walk with love and reverence. —Henry David Thoreau*

**Enter**

To enter
a step must first
be taken.
Listen to the crooked
creek as it babbles.
Honor the stream
of your soul.

Dare to
dip your feet
in the moving
current of life.
The invitation
awaits you,
so does the river.

While trust
must lead,
walk with love.
There are no
guarantees
for what awaits
cannot yet be seen.

So with the wind
at my back and
courage in my step,
I enter the narrow path
that is my life.
May it lead me to new
places of self-discovery.

—Wendi Romero

*For your reflection:* Walk with love and reverence.

*Life can only be understood backwards, but it must be lived forwards.*
—*Soren Kierkegaard*

## Reflections

When I reflect
God reflects back to me

all of creation in the
mirror of his turning hand.

An enduring presence,
an all-encompassing love,

looking back at me
through the looking glass.

Finding God, who is truth,
is to discover my own truth.

But, if I have been in error,
my first step toward truth

is in humility to discover
my own mistakes—

moments of reflection,
a bridge to healing

between the old story
and the new one,

waiting to be written from
the fragments of my life.

—Wendi Romero

*For your reflection*: What are you learning by reflecting on your life?

*You must learn one thing. The world was made to be free in.*
*—David Whyte*

## Curious Freedom

A rebel, you say.
No wonder it has taken so long.

The soft freedom of curiosity waits
to break the rebellious shell.

Born to be enveloped by
the caress of wind—
watch, listen, and breathe in wisdom.

No one needs to know the tension held,
the muse tickling your thoughts.

Pierce the misty screen between the veils
and break free.

Be Alive!

—Deidre Montgomery

*For your reflection:* What does your inner muse say to you?

*Joy and sorrow are sisters, they reside in the same house.*
—*Macrina Wiederkehr*


## The Eternal Classroom

My soul weeps,
so much sadness.
The mystery beckons to the why,
where there are no clear answers.

We do not escape suffering.
It draws us deeper to God's presence.
We know in the depths of sorrow and suffering
Love prevails.

We sit in the loneliness,
where memories flow with tears,
knowing there is great purpose in
the joys and sorrows.

In life she taught us how to be more than we are.
In dying she taught us to love deeper.

—Pat Low


***For your reflection***: Treasure the gift of friends and family each day.

*Set me as a seal upon thine heart, as a seal upon thine arm, for love is stronger than death.* —*Song of Solomon 8:6*

## Visible Sign of a Divine Grace

My husband, Frank, and I have received the blessing of a long marriage. We met as college freshman in the very first class we ever took at LSU. Our first date was to study for our first English test. We went to the library, studied for about an hour, then went to Hopper's Drive-In for a hamburger and a coke. We never went back to the library. Instead, we talked all afternoon until time to go home. On June 2, 2020, we celebrated our fifty-fourth wedding anniversary. As many of you know, when a couple stays married, many pleasures, differences, wonders, changes, upsets, tears, growth, and blessings occur. It takes regard, kindness, flexibility, acceptance, spirit, and prayer to stay together and have a meaningful relationship.

To collect my thoughts concerning this topic, I looked up the word, "Sacrament." The definition includes ritual, rite of passage, a visible sign of divine grace. The most touching for me is *a visible sign of divine grace.* I thought of our wedding rings, our daughter, our grandchildren, and the spirit between us that is still alive and active. Perhaps the best grace is that we like each other, have fun, enjoy time together, both quiet and alone; as well as being together with others, laughing and enjoying friendships.

On the other side, there is the reality that marriage is not easy. Joseph Campbell, mythologist and philosopher, said, "Marriage is an ordeal; two different individuals come together and attempt to find a way to become one." This is where another significant quality enters the marriage: commitment.

—Sidney Creaghan

*For your reflection:* Choice is the engine of life. Take time to reflect upon an important choice you have made, whether it was a winsome one or a regrettable one, and write about it.

## Not Myself

Disconnected
Distracted
Going through the motions
And then not so much

Getting lost
In minutia
In books
In procrastination

Not present
To myself
To others
To much of anything

Irascible
Irritated by every little thing
More sarcastic than usual
Every nerve exposed

Out of patience
Out of compassion
Swimming in a sea of not caring
The blues or grief?

—Trudy Gomez

*For your reflection:* What do you do when you feel out of sorts and not yourself?

*Reading and reflecting on Cynthia Bourgeault's book, The Wisdom*
*Way of Knowing: Reclaiming an Ancient Tradition to Awaken the Heart,*
*brought forth the following thoughts:*

**Searching for the Path of Wisdom**

Here we sit in our original containers,
seeking that wisdom that will bring
our whole being into balance,
so that the rhythm of our lives will play with such clarity
that our vision cannot help but widen.

As I unfold the next roadmap to wholeness,
I plan to take the most direct route.
My strategies in the past often led to dead ends.
Awakening begins with listening to my body,
allowing its wisdom to speak.

How do I intuit this wisdom?
I get right next to the origin, the center of each cell
that participates in the knowing—as I am known.
My transformation is a be-coming.

Coming home begins when my mind seeks understanding.
As I be-friend the body, moving in work, play, and prayer,
a bridge is built, allowing me to be present to the
re-creation occurring in me.

How do I serve as the midwife to this co-creation?
Allow the aliveness to come to full consciousness
by surrendering to the growth occurring from life experiences,
as body-mind-spirit trusts in the guidance within.
Am I ready to surrender to this freedom?
It takes a fearless attitude to let the aliveness flourish.
There may be the illusion that I am "giving up control,"
when in reality, surrender gives me the gift of not needing control.

Creation calls out to my heart, inviting my conscience to
recognize the patterns of aliveness in all things.
"I see" and I begin to dance to the Divine Rhythms in the now.

A phrase from a hymn arises: "Come into Love's presence, singing of
joy." Centering prayer awakens my heart, leading it within. Today I can
delight in exactly where and who I am, thanks be to God.

—Betty Landreneau

*For your reflection:* What words invite you to ponder the aspects of
your own transformation?

# Legacy and Influence

Photo by Wendi Romero

*There are different places on our property that call me to relax, to remember, to rest.*

**The Sound of the Pines**

Sometimes, sounds of the pines next to our home speak to me in their swaying, dance-like moves. It's a sound that speaks through wind in the pine needles and limbs of these giants. Sometimes, the wind whistles, and in other moments, it howls like a wolf.

I wonder if these giants, likewise, spoke to my father in the winds that blew in his time. Did they thank him for planting them and allowing them their lives?

Perhaps he once thanked them for bringing beauty, pine scents, and majesty to this property that he loved, and that I now live on and love. I often sit near them to hear them as my father did.

Sometimes, the raindrops fall on the wings of a hawk that I see high in the pines, as his expert eyes search for "life food." But the hawk is safe in the pine trees' branches that protect him, especially near the trunk, which reaches very high above the ground. He can watch through the rain, and to the ground, at the place where trunk and branch meet. I believe he feels protected there!

I love to spending time watching the activity and remembering times past with these giants ... and with my Father.

—Cheryl Delahoussaye

*For your reflection*: Are there special places near your home that call to you? If so, how do these places make you feel?

*The mystery of human existence lies not in just staying alive but in finding something to live for.* —Fyodor Dostoyevsky

## Her Hands

Holding Mom's hands, I realize
I don't have to be a palm reader.
No need to know her future.
The better story: her journey to now.

Undying love coursing through her veins
leaving a visible roadmap on each hand.
Slender fingers
lifting spirits
holding pain
weaving joy through our lives.
Her knobby knuckles once nimble
always attentive to the handiwork,
her children.

I fold her hands in her lap.
Finally, at rest.

—Michelle Lafleur MacFadyen

*For your reflection*: Are you living out who you were created to be?
What's holding you back?

*Heavenly Father, use my living as a legacy for your glory and the enrichment of others.*

## Will I Be Remembered?

"Will I be remembered?" A question my Dad asked me two days before he left this earth for his final home. Do all people who are transitioning ask that question? There were other questions that came before that one, and here are a few.

He asked if my mom would be ok? Would she have enough money? He asked if my sister would be ok? He asked if he would know his mother, his father, and his brother, Leroy? Both, his parents and brother, were deceased years before.

Then the "Will I be remembered" question came by surprise. I answered each question to the best of my ability as we stared into each other's eyes searching for the truth. I took my time, speaking slowly, never breaking down, staying strong in the Lord, and telling him all the reasons he absolutely would be remembered.

When all was said, he smiled and said, "Life was good, huh?" Then he fell asleep, resting peacefully for the first time in months. He finally quit fighting his death, but now accepting it, as his time drew near. A few weeks before, in a panicked state, I asked him if he was still afraid to die. I'll never forget what he cried out. It actually changed the way I think about those preparing to move to their final home. In anguish, he said, "No, I'm just not ready to leave ya'll!" It was then that I realized how our loved ones suffer, all in the name of love, just as Jesus did for us.

My final gift to him was to speak at his funeral. I never dreamed I'd be able to, but God gave me the strength to complete this last task.

This is what I wrote, and read aloud:

"I'm studying the life of King David, the man after God's own heart. It quickly became clear to me that David, just like Dad, and just like me, made mistakes and was not perfect. We're human and bound to make them. Anyone who knew my Dad knew how ornery and hard-headed he was. It was his way or no way, and he always had to have the last word.

But, just like David, he could make you laugh, he could make you cry, he could amuse you, he could disappoint you. He could make you want to be just like him at times, and nothing like him at others. It's so easy to put our finger on all the mistakes our parents might have made. I'm quite sure my own children can name many. But will he be remembered? This was important to him. What legacy did Dad leave? What about the things that he did do right?

The values and beliefs I hold today grew as a result of being raised by him. I was five years old when he married my mom. He had a strong faith in the Lord, along with a strong love of family, friends, and life. He did for others, never expecting anything in return. He worked hard to provide for his family, sometimes three jobs at a time, for us to live very comfortably. He had a sense of humor, even in his darkest hours. And, during the four years when his health was declining and he was losing his independence, he sometimes could still make you laugh.

Sure, he made mistakes, we all do. But from my Dad's example, I have become the person and parent I am today. He and my mom loved unconditionally, which got me through some very dark times, and they always welcomed me home."

I now believe we can all be a man or woman after God's own heart. I certainly hope that I have strived to live such a life worthy of being remembered for it all … for being too loud, for my versions of the good, the bad, and the ugly. I've always wanted to give others hope and be a positive light, but we all fall short at times. The choices we make now will impact how others see us when we're gone.

—Denise Broussard

*For your reflection:* Do you wonder if you'll be remembered once you leave this earth? What legacy do you want to leave behind?

## Bits of Sand

Walking along the water's edge
Watching my grandson swishing sand between his fingers.
Shells litter the tide's edge.

Some intact, others in broken bits
Still others ground into even smaller bits by wave action.
The scattered bits that are eventually turned to even smaller
bits of sand.

I pick up the intact, the broken, and the sand
Each grain unique but lost in the many.
I examine and wonder

What will I leave behind as life takes its toll?
Will there be bits of me to remember, experience, hold,
Like the bits of sand that lingers to skin?

—Trudy Gomez

*For your reflection:* How do you imagine you will be remembered?

## Build

Build in me a new spirit, Lord,
instill your path of love and right.
I would put on your essence of goodness
as a cloak wrapped around my soul.

Going deeper than external,
beyond what is seen, I welcome your love
into every level of my being;
it brings me back to life.

Love builds a home within the Spirit
with a door that welcomes all.
Those who choose to enter
are served with grace and gratitude.

Such a home is stronger than anything
built by hand.
Even castles rise and fall,
but the love of God is eternal,
built on an unshakable foundation.

Cities and fortresses may crumble.
That made by mankind can fall
but the firmness of the love of God,
God's love,
will never pass away.

—B. D. Lowry

*For your reflection*: I welcome a home of love within me.

*Inspired by a vision, a "seeing" in prayer circle in Sacred Center a few years ago.*

## The Grandmothers

The soft chime gathers us in.
The reader's voice gives suggestion.
My eyes close but I see,
I see the ancestors, the grandmothers.
They come alive from the shadows
Leaning in
Embracing us
Love is made known.
Their interest intent
Their eyes alight
They peer into the center at each one present.
I feel the breath of their wisdom.
I hear the unified voice "Through you."

—Trudy Gomez

*For your reflection*: Have you ever experienced a *Communion of Saints* or a union with your ancestors?

# Longing and Loving

Photo by Trudy Gomez

*You find peace not by rearranging the circumstances of your life, but by realizing who you are at the deepest level. —Eckhart Tolle*

## Landslide of the Heart

When I stop yearning
for what was
never mine
and start wanting
what I already have,
my time has come.

There's no way to
prepare for a landslide
of the heart,
but just to trust
that one day I will
land on my feet again.

Until I find my way,
my inner soil
shifts with great force,
the earth below me
quakes, and my inner
geography crumbles.

When my dust settles,
my wanting will
finally be over.
For what I yearned
has been found,
for what I wanted

I learned I already had.

—Wendi Romero

***For your reflection***: At your deepest level, may you realize who you truly are.

*Everyone says love hurts, but that's not true. Loneliness hurts. Rejection hurts. Losing someone hurts. Envy hurts. Everyone gets these things confused with love, but in reality, love is the only thing in this world that covers up all the pain and makes someone feel wonderful again. Love is the only thing that does not hurt. —Liam Neeson*

## Valentine, What's Love Got to Do with It?

Love.
A simple four-letter word.
Not perfect and wrapped
in a pretty box with a bow.
But, it's a beautiful thing.

Love.
Fills your heart
with so much joy.
It feels as though it
will burst wide open.
At other times, the heart,
so heavy with grief,
feels like it will break in two.

Looking at someone you love,
your heart skips a beat with passion.
Then, in the heat of a moment,
it stops beating for a second
with so much anger and hurt
for that same loved one.

Love is easy.
Love is challenging.
Love is all you ever imagined,
and so worth the effort.
We want to love
and be loved.
Yet, sometimes fear it.

Love can heal our pain,
but fear of getting hurt
stands in the way.

Do we love
without expecting
anything in return?
Do we love others
as God loves us
unconditionally?

We love and lose
family and friends
who meant everything.
They changed our lives
and were there for us
when we needed them most.

Love.
Confusing, with mixed messages.
Other times, clear as a bell,
no questions asked.
Learn by experiencing.
Two steps forward,
three steps back.
Embrace all meanings
and all feelings.

Knowing it is
God's purpose for us.
Our greatest gift and
every heart's desire.
Everyone wants it.
Everyone needs to love.
Everyone wants to be loved.

Love has everything to do
about everything.

So praise the Lord and pass the chocolates!

—Denise Broussard

*For your reflection*: There certainly is true love here on earth, but
can you just imagine His pure love when we meet, face to face? Take a
breath and breathe that in.

## He Said

He said:
I hold you in the palm of my hand,
You are held in love.
I love you in your messiness,
In your negativity and your cynicism.
You are enough!

He said:
When you have no self-love,
I love you.
When you have no self-appreciation,
I love you.
You are enough!

He said:
I Am bigger than what you can contain.
I Am more expansive than you can conceive.
In my breath is love, joy, compassion.
I Am the abundance that surrounds you.
I Am the source of your freedom.

He said:
I hold you in the palm of my hand,
Allow the embrace,
Allow the love,
Allow the peace,
You are enough!

—Trudy Gomez

*For your reflection*: What hinders you from believing when God says
you are enough just as you are? What helps you believe it?

*The truth may set you free, but first it will shatter the safe, sweet way you live.* —Sue Monk Kidd

## Holy Longing

Who among us hasn't experienced a slowly dawning truth of how our life is not being lived in accordance to our soul's yearning? Sometimes it is such a slow dawning that it takes decades to be manifest, even in small ways. Sometimes it is a sudden realization that "my life no longer works in this form." I have experienced both and in-between. Many of you have as well.

As a woman born in the south in the 1940s and reared with the standards and beliefs of a small southern town of the 1950s, I have a code of behavior that is embedded in my being, in my cellular structure. I like that I am polite and greet people with a welcoming smile and, often, a hug. There are many values I still hold that make me grateful for having been nurtured in that time and place. I have begun to embrace that I am a small-town woman at heart and small town can't be wished or polished out of me. However, I will say, I have so many "ladies don't ..." admonitions in those same cellular structures, that I have spent many years persistently unlearning those restrictive codes.

By the end of my thirties, my shattering moved in and would no longer be ignored. I certainly tried. I may not have been living a sweet life, but it was safe and not really *unsweet*. I was working to hold on to any fragment or scrap of my "old" self, almost like I was spinning apart, and didn't understand why or what to do about it. What was going on? Was I losing my mind?

This was a very confusing time, because no one had ever spoken to me of there being something called "self," *besides* those other identities of mother and wife, daughter and sister, friend and employee, aunt, cousin, neighbor, and so on. I never experienced a hint from anyone and so I came to a truth that only my longing brought about. *There was a whole that was me and not parsed out as the other identities.* Yes— me, mine, along with those other things, maybe even before those other things. Be me, first, so I can show up authentically as my gift to relationships with others.

I tried so very hard to keep my new realizations contained. If I could stay in my lane, I could maintain this life. My life was pretty good. I didn't want to exchange what I knew for all that unknown "boogey-man" stuff. But, I was not good at staying in my lane.

No one I knew was speaking about such things as "finding yourself" or a longing for … what exactly? What was my longing? I could not have put into words my general disquiet than I could understand what was happening. Anything I thought and put into words sounded whiney, ungrateful, and well, crazy.

Many people have made "finding yourself" a cliché that attempts to make this much-needed awakening a joke, or at the very least, unnecessary. Mine was so totally necessary, and I can assure you it was no joke.

I could find mentors only in books at that particular time in my life. Women and men were writing about this awakening, this longing for self, and I found some really wonderful mentors as authors. I have since discovered many exquisite mentors. Many are known to me personally and others are from excellent books. All have helped me on this never ending journey.

We have a holy longing around each new phase, each new level of awareness, that is necessary to our growth as a spiritual and loving human being. I am grateful to find, in the respites, a sweeter life than I could have dreamed.

I am so very thankful to have found women and men who recognize that we need to be self-aware, we need an *"us"* in the world so that we can bring the best of who we are to our experience, and therefore, help each person follow their own holy longing. I think we are all mentors in some way, and we are here to help one another.

—Avis Lyons LeBlanc

*For your reflection*: Who might need your help with their Holy Longing? Search out mentors if you need help with you own.

## Love Came Running

Love came running
Not caring that I had gone astray
Rejoicing in my return
Welcoming unconditionally
Embracing all of me
Covering all the brokenness with new garments
Kisses and tears washing away all the hurts
Love rejoices over me.

—Trudy Gomez

*For your reflection:* Allow yourself to be caught up in God's loving embrace.

## Rhythms of Life

After listening to drum rhythms, I pondered what variety of rhythms had been a part of my life.

Feel the rhythm of the drums.
Does it match the beat of your heart?
There is a wildness and excitement that grows,
nourished by the life-beat within.

Many rhythms dance us along the path to freedom.
Feel the measured beats of others,
your own carefully crafted rhythm,
unfiltered chaotic sounds even your inner critic cannot squash.
A yearning uses these sounds to give birth to
"What if …?"

If you stop the beat/dance, the urge to move arises again.
Each beginning re-awakens a burning desire to celebrate,
joining your rhythm to others, melding and co-creating
the ever new you.

—Betty Landreneau

*For your reflection*: Identify the various rhythms that have been part of your life.

## Stranger

What do I see when I look in the mirror?
Do I see myself as God's good creation?
Do I see the potential of me?
Do I see the miracle of me?
Do I see what God sees?

When I look in the mirror, I sometimes catch a glimpse
and want to avert my eyes
from things I don't want to see
beyond the wrinkles, the sags, the bulges,
to the dreams not realized,
the potential not tapped.
Saddened by
The baggage I have carried that separates me
The things from which I avert my eyes:
The wounded child
The fearful girl
The angry, unforgiving one
The parts of me that I thought had healed.
Like looking in a fun-house mirror!
A distorted picture of me?

I ask, is that stranger there, is that the real me?
Am I just a reflection, a shadow of who I am supposed to be?
When I look into the mirror, what do I see?
Do I see myself as God's beloved?
Do I see myself as holy and pleasing to God?
Do I see myself as sacred and worthy?
Do I respect that I am these things and act accordingly?
Where did I get so off track?
not seeing the divine spark within?
and that the Holy Spirit resides in me?
Failing to acknowledge that I am loved, cherished as God's unique
creation

Seen beyond the surface …
Seen through Love's eyes.

—Trudy Gomez

*For your reflection*: Lord, help me see myself and others not through a mirror darkly, but through eyes of love. Help me see that "it is good" when I look at myself and the world around me. Take away my negativity. Help me when I cling to my insecurities and doubts about myself and don't live the life you planned for me to see; not the distorted reflection, but to say thank you, and to live as if I truly believe that I am your beloved. Amen.

# Nature and Nurture

Photo by Wendi Romero

*All streams flow to the sea. The water returns to where the streams began.* —Ecclesiastes 1:7

## Until We Part

Let us move toward
each other
before we move apart.

Soon enough the path splits
but having shared it
makes all the difference.

Crossing the divide between
deep south and northern lights,
I move closer to meet

a drifting orphan of ice
just broken off from its
melting mother glacier—

a swimming sculpture,
azure as it floats to greet me
on the rocky shore of my life.

As I kneel to meet the cold
multifaceted mystery,
it drips and sticks to my skin.

We hold on to each other
as long as we can before
my hand begins to burn.

It's only for a short time,
this meeting between me
and a chunk of frozen sea,

so I raised it high like
a consecrated chalice
and offered it back.

It must go its way
and I go mine.
All must return,

every drop that ever was.

—Wendi Romero

*For your reflection*: Observe the transforming nature of something as it changes form, sometimes in your very hands.

*I have found that spending just five minutes out in nature can reframe my perspective of a situation. The key for me is to take a few deep inhales and exhales, then look with relaxed eyes at a detail of nature and allow my mind to empty and float in this relaxed space.*

## Connections to God

While out walking my dog, I stopped because I was puzzled by what I saw. There, beneath the oak tree, was a leaf just spinning in mid-air. I gazed at this single suspended leaf, hanging and spinning, from what I thought was the branch just overhead. The leaf appeared to be floating in the air, yet kept spinning in place, moved by the wind. As the leaf danced and spun in place, I marveled how it was like a ballerina spinning on one toe. I searched and looked for a thread or some connection with the branches above or the ground below. Surely something spinning in place as such was tethered to a solid object? No matter from which angle I looked, I was never able to discern its connection to a larger object above or below that explained its security as it spun in place propelled by the wind. I thought, Ah! This must be how we humans are connected to God and the Earth, connected by the invisible thread of God's love.

That is the only explanation I could come up with. Perhaps next time I will just feel and experience the awe of what I am seeing and let my mind relax into the wonder of the mystery in front of me. There is not always an answer to the question my mind poses.

The "I" that wants the answer is not who I am. That is my mind seeking to "figure things out." I am not my mind. I am light, I am an aspect of God—or rather, an aspect of God who is in me.

—Lissee Spiller

*For your reflection:* Pay attention to the little details that surround you as you go about your day. Make time to relax, breathe deeply, then perhaps your eyes will open to your connection to something larger than yourself. Your connection to the bigger picture of life or your part in the bigger picture of God's design for this life.

*You can't stop the waves, but you can learn to surf.* —*Kabat-Zinn*

## Peaceful Yet Powerful

My morning ritual,
a walk on the beach
as the sun is rising.
I pray and ponder in awe.

Sights, smells, feelings,
all senses come alive.
Blue green, the color of the sea,
absent of any seaweed.
I can literally smell it.

White foam from the waves
crashing on the shoreline.
Waves washing up seashells
for me to gather.
I truly see it with different eyes.

Backdrop is breathtaking—
a blue sky scattered with clouds.
All shapes and forms throughout
as I can feel His presence.

God's creation,
artist of the universe,
speaking to me in ways
He knows I will understand.
He brings peace to my mind
and my spirit, so I thank Him.

The smell of seawater, intoxicating.
The feel of sand between
my toes, exhilarating.
The sound of waves reminding me that

water has such a peaceful element.
But don't mess with Mother Nature,
water is also very powerful.

Picking up seashells along the way.
Watching seagulls flying overhead.
Sometimes they run to escape the waves.
I think of God's words, "Look at the birds
of the air, they do not sow or reap
or store away in barns, and yet
your Heavenly Father feeds them.
Are you not much more valuable than these?"

Finally, I believe I am valuable.
Stormy waters will come, troubling
thoughts too. Emotional waves
will hit my spirit, but My Lord
will protect me from life's difficulties
that toss me around.
Even through powerful waters,
I find a calm sea of peace.
My Lord is living water,
peaceful, yet powerful.

"God is our refuge and strength,
an ever-present help in trouble.
Therefore, we will not fear,
though the earth gives way,
mountains fall into the heart
of the sea, though it's waters
roar and foam."

—Denise Broussard

*quotes from Matthew: 6:26 and Psalm: 46

*For your reflection:* Are you ready to start relaxing with nature, even
when difficulties arise in your life or the lives of your loved ones?

*They who dwell in the ends of the earth, stand in awe of Your signs; you make the dawn and the sunsets shout for joy. —Psalm 65:8*

## The Gift in Sunsets

Great music playing,
dinner on the grill.
Conversations shared with
laughter filling the balcony.
Delicious appetizers consumed
while hearts are filled with gratitude.

Our ritual at the beach,
patiently waiting for sunset.
The same scene daily—
we never get tired of it.
Overlooking the bay,
the same sailboat always
in the exact sacred place
as we journey around the sun.

The sun is high in the sky,
the bay appears dark.
As the sun starts to set,
it turns into a huge red ball.
Water reflecting like a mirror,
light striking it as we see
a long light path
to the end of the horizon.
Breathtaking.

We all stop in awe
at the beauty of amazing grace.
We watch as the sun's light
make the water sparkle.
The light's path is dead center
on the boat, making it literally glow.

The sky is unbelievably colorful.
Violet, blue, yellow, orange, red.
Nature does speak to the heart
if only we stop and listen.
As the water reflects the light,
we have our quiet reflection
of beauty and mystery of life.

As we watch the sun set,
light fades, and darkness appears.
Our bodies breathe deeper.
All cares and stress fade away
as does the light.
Now the stars come out.
Another way of God
drawing us to Him
at the end of each day.

—Denise Broussard

*For your reflection:* From the rising of the sun to its setting, can you remember times when God seemed to be speaking to your heart? Do you take the time to praise Him for these gifts?

*The Spirit prays in us with sighs too deep for words.*
—*Romans 8:26*


## Wild Splendor

I sit within arm's reach of an elk as he enjoys lush foraging along the edges of this narrow piece of the Hoh River, and he isn't at all concerned about my presence. He is where he belongs, and I am just another piece of his land.

We are staying in the campground of the Hoh Rainforest in the Olympic National Park on the edge of the Hoh River, a 50-mile-long, wild, deep, and ancient river. This is one of many gravel bars created by the rush of water during the snow-melt. Here the river is only puddles of water amid the gravel and buff soil. We can walk across it at this time of year, jumping puddles and navigating the piles of trees and branches pushed here during the torrents caused by the melting snow at the top of Mount Olympus.

I can imagine the roaring torrent at that time. Wide and beautiful glacier water created when rock, in its rush downstream, is ground into what's called glacial flour that colors the water a milky, pale blue. Glacier water has this "flour" suspended in it, neither sinking nor rising, just remains suspended in the water. It is a very ethereal color, white/blue unlike any other water I've ever seen. Otherworldly.

I love living among these Roosevelt Elk herds that walk freely in the campground and mingle with us easily. This is their home but they don't seem to mind sharing. The cows and young bulls are frisky and play as you would expect any young to do. The fuzzy antlers of the young bulls make me think of our teen boys and their peach fuzz. A spirited bunch!

Our stay within the Olympic National Park has shown me a wildness that I don't encounter often. First, Mora Campground with its Hansel and Gretel darkness and distorted trees on their stilts, having grown over hundreds of years from atop a decaying log, creating fairy houses beneath their roots.

Rialto Beach, my favorite place in the continental United States, with its wild ocean and bones of ancient trees guarding the beach and the Sea Stacks rearing up from the ocean looking like ancient rock formations.

Now, the Hoh Rainforest. Another wild place where trees are shaped into bent backs or tall giants with long beards. This entire area seems like a Grimm's Fairy Tale, except it isn't frightening. It just feels ancient, and much of it is. The Hoh Valley from the park boundary to Mount Olympus looks much like it has for 5,000 years, according to the literature.

This area makes me long for a wildness that I can't even articulate because I have never experienced it. I don't even know how to frame that wildness. Does wild mean free? Is my wild self so hidden it thinks it's normal to be this buttoned down?

The elk doesn't even know it's wild; it just is. I just am, too. I am just wild, too. As a part of nature as the elk is part of nature, as the banana slug is part of nature, as the giant tree is part of nature, so am I.

I think getting back to nature is much more difficult than it should be. I have to go into a forest or other "natural place" to be "in" nature instead of recognizing, coming to the realization that I am as much nature as the grass beneath my feet and the branches of the tree I pass beneath. This has become a new quest for me: to *know* that we are all nature and not separate from nature, and we are all one within that. I am so domesticated that I don't even know myself as nature. I desire to *know* it in my being.

—Avis Lyons LeBlanc

*For your reflection*: Do you have a quest? Perhaps you too are seeking your wildness, your natural spirit.

**From Psalm 84**

I resonate with the Source of All,
heart and soul resound like a plucked string,
perfectly tuned to the Divine.

Would that each moment bring such attunement!
Yet many times I grow slack,
pitch falling short as faith falters,
dampening and dimming who I am.

Do not turn from me, oh God,
for then I cannot clearly hear your call.
Hide not your face from me.
I grow deaf and blind.

My soul stirs, a voice within
whispers truth: Who has turned away?
The voice of mystery replies:
I will never leave you.

I falter, I return
to the Eternal One,
the source of all lovingkindness,
my strength and my stronghold.

I rise, I find your strength fills my being,
singing in me your song of life,
resonating again with all of creation,
joyously breathing your Being.

—B. D. Lowry

*For your reflection:* I resonate with all of creation.

*It's so easy to look around and see what's wrong. It takes patience and wisdom to see what's right. —Melody Beattie*

## The Great Wisdom of Nature

We are having our first warm, sunny day in quite a while. I grab my shears and hoe, and head out to my butterfly garden. Deep in my heart is the hope that the Monarchs will return this year. Last May, we had almost a hundred pupae, and I had the thrill of seeing the Monarchs hatch out and reveal their incomparable beauty against the rough, green wood of my cabin … before they winged away. All summer I saw a few, in and out of the garden.

But now, my butterfly garden looks like a sort of sodden green sculpture created by a trickster. A plant that my dad called "vetch" has grown over everything, leaving a green space filled with lumps. Coming out of the lumps are the dead sticks that were last year's butterfly milkweed, the only plant that Monarch in the pupae stage like.

Murmuring, "Every journey begins with one step," I walk into the garden and begin pulling the green vetch away from the lumps. Beneath the dead twigs of the old butterfly milkweed, new plants are clustered. There are at least four of them in the wreckage of each of last year's plants. I realize that the loathsome vetch has protected the young plants from the cold. I stand for a moment, thinking, *Mother Earth, Gaia, your wisdom is ancient and profound*. I am filled with hope for a new season of Monarchs, but I can only prepare. I can't control their coming.

If you saw my garden the day after my adventure into it, you would not see a lot of changes. It does not look landscaped at all. I have uncovered some of the little plants and given them a dose of very weak liquid fertilizer. I have cut back a portion of the dead growth. It's going to be a slow process, like nature herself.

I remember one season seeking help with my butterfly garden. A young man stood on the labyrinth and said, "Well, I would just weed eat the whole thing." That's when I knew that as a gardener, and not a landscaper, I would have to be content with what others saw as a mess. I love the pristine, colorful flower bed that is mulched and clean. But sometimes that is not what is needed, and I must work slowly with nature's plan.

In my garden, according to nature, everything is going according to plan. And She is so much wiser than I am.

—Lyn Holley Doucet

*For your reflection:* Look around and see the gifts of nature. Open your heart to her messiness and her abundance.

# Prayer and Meditation

Photo by Denise Broussard

## In Touch

Keeping "in touch" with God keeps me balanced. I can get kind of cuckoo if I don't. I can let the stuff of everyday life pull me off balance. Sometimes I just have to give myself a time-out!

I will turn to zoning out in front of the TV, escaping in the pages of a book, stress eating, shopping as therapy, or pulling the covers over my head. These are all forms of avoidance; they constrict my life and relationships, and they are temporary fixes and in the long run only prolong the cuckoos.

Staying in balance, being centered and in harmony with my Creator is like taking deep cleansing breaths. Meditation, prayer, Eucharist, scripture help re-center me and put things in perspective, but I sometimes use them as a last resort instead of a first resort. They help me to be mindful and to remember the promises of God. They help support and nurture my life in Christ! They refocus me on joy and restore my glass-filling-up attitude. They help build up my faith.

—Trudy Gomez

*For your reflection:* Pray: Holy Spirit, Holy Breath, it is through your prompting, your breathing life into me, that I can be present to Mercy and Love. *"To the one who is able to keep you (me) from stumbling and to present you unblemished and exultant, in the presence of his glory, to the only God, our savior, through Jesus Christ our Lord be glory, majesty, power, and authority from ages past, now, and for ages to come. Amen." (Jude 17:20-25)*

*Life can unfold in the most interesting ways. Yet, we can still achieve our dreams. Enjoy the journey.*

## I Asked

When I held my son for the first time, another woman was watching me closely. His biological mother. We stood two feet apart while I held her child. She told me prior to giving birth that she knew that she could not hold him after birth, or she would never be able to release him to me.

Initially, when the nurse arrived with the new baby, she was determined to lay him in the biological mother's arms. The biological mother repeatedly asked her to give him to me. The nurse did not seem to be processing this and continually tried to lay the baby in her arms. I finally said, "GIVE ME THE BABY." It's like she snapped out of some trance and finally relinquished him to me. What a close call that was … and how grateful I am that I intervened and spoke up, or I might never had held my son, Luc.

My journey to motherhood had been a very long road. My body was not properly holding my pregnancies, despite the fact that there was apparently nothing wrong with me, biologically.

Many of my friends and acquaintances were getting pregnant and having healthy babies, yet it did not bother me. Friends would ask if it affected me when I saw another pregnant woman. It never ever did, which seemed strange, even to me. I continually felt and verbalized to those that asked, that I was clear that it was obviously their journey and how could I judge that? I knew that for whatever reason, that this was my journey. And it would unfold as it was meant to. Those words just fell from my lips, without thought.

So, after attempting fertility treatments for a year (to speed things up), we still were not pregnant. I finally looked at my husband and said, "We want a family. There are lots of ways that families are made. Would you be open to adopting?" While it took some time for him to adapt to the idea, he trusted and loved me and thus agreed to start the adoption process. The adoption process is lengthy and time consuming, just to clarify. And just for the record, Catholic Social Services told us we were too old to adopt. It was the first place we contacted. We were shocked and hurt and frankly very confused with this information. I was forty. So be it.

We ended up "listing," as it is called, with two private adoption agencies. I submitted biography binders to both (sort of a selling tool for prospective parents that pregnant mothers look through to pick a family. All mandatory.)

Shockingly, in 2 short weeks we got our first call that we had been selected by a mother! Unreal ... I am to understand that this is not the norm. I was over the moon! 2 weeks, I could hardly BELIEVE it! So many people wait so long for that call! The biological mother was due in 6 weeks.

However, she went into labor 4 weeks early and our precious son was born. And ... let me add that the minute I hung up the phone with the first adoption attorney, the 2$^{nd}$ adoption attorney called me to say that he had twins for me. (Side note: I had ALWAYS wanted twins!!) That we had been selected by a mother, I was both shocked and thrilled. I said, "I'll take them!" I did explain to him that we were on our way to New Orleans to pick up my baby from the other adoption attorney. He chuckled and told me that he would not place them with another family until he heard back from me. He asked me to call him in a week, and congratulated me on becoming a mother. Looking back, I considered that a very kind gesture to us. Knowing full well that there was a 90% chance that we would not take the twins once I had a newborn in my arms! (Think triplets!)

Driving home with my premature (5 pound) baby days later was a nerve-racking event. He was so tiny! And, I was completely unprepared—in all ways. I did not have a diaper, a crib, a book, nothing. We had no notice! While we drove to pick up our son in New Orleans, my precious friends got together all of the things I would need for a new baby.

They were in stacks since I did not have a nursey yet—the diaper changing stack, the feeding stack, the clothing stack, etc .... It was a shambles despite their efforts. To say the first month was pandemonium is an understatement. There is a reason God gives you 9 months to prepare for a new baby, FYI. Not only is it a physical adjustment, it is a HUGE emotional adjustment!

Our son did not sleep much (it took him 18 months to sleep through the night) and did not seem comfortable in his skin initially. I intuitively saw and felt that he needed 100% of me. So, I called the 2nd adoption attorney and told him that I would not be taking the twins. Part of my heart broke releasing them, but I'm not sure we could handle triplets with NO WARNING OR PREPARATION. (I'm pretty sure my husband was beyond relieved).

The rest of my story reads like this … LOVE, LOVE, LOVE, LOVE.

I could bore you with painful details of the reality of creating our family, or create a dramatic story of how hard it was. But the reality is that we just put our heads down and continued to dive into it … daily. Laser focus. Full commitment of time and energy. A family. A child. What could POSSIBLY be more important? (To us, anyway.)

So to those out there who might not be getting what you wished for, or hoped for, or dreamed of, or are working for … I say to you, respect your journey. There are so many gifts along the way when you must encounter and rise above adversity and struggle. And if things don't gel and move forward, reevaluate and see if God is trying to redirect you. Because usually … if things are not coming together and it is continually difficult, it can be a sign that God sees a different direction for you. One that will expand you, if you allow it. It can be hard to shift gears, to change the landscape of your dreams. But plug in to your inner voice, your higher self, and listen. Feel it … see where he wants you to go.

—Ann Kergan

*For your reflection:* Your journey may not be what you imagined and hoped for, but the outcome can be just as beautiful. Listen to your heart and to God, and let the rest fall into place. Continue to pray and ASK FOR WHAT YOU WANT.

*Prayer is powerful. It can heal, prayer can give, and it can change lives.*
*—Shane DeCreshio*


## The Power of Prayer

On April 18, 2018, I was in a horrific, near-fatal car accident. A young lady with six children in her boyfriend's car plowed through a red light and T-boned me. I was the only one injured; no one in her car was injured.

I never saw the car hit me. When I opened my eyes, first responders were already in my car. The jaws of life were used to extricate me from my car. I remember very little. A week and five major surgeries later, I was just finding out the details of my wreck.

I had broken 38 bones, punctured my lungs, and slivered my spleen, all due to the blunt-force trauma to my abdomen and body.

I had to tap into my faith, remind myself to give thanks for all things, good and not good. I reminded myself to be grateful to be alive. Grateful for the care of doctors and nurses during this terrifying time. The source of my strength and comfort came from all the love, prayers, and kindness of my Sacred Heart sisters, my family, friends, and the community united in prayer for my recovery. All this helped me cope.

One of my daily prayers, short and sweet, was given to me by Don Briggs, who himself had been in a near- fatal accident. The prayer reads, "Father, today help me to get a little better. I trust in you, Jesus."

I was in the hospital and rehab for two months, in a wheelchair for almost six months. I had very little use of my left leg. Nearly two years later, I have made almost a full recovery. I've returned to exercising, swimming, lifting weights, and Pilates. My pelvic doctor believes my muscles are what held me together. With the power of prayers, I recovered.

One of the saddest memories after my accident was the fact I had to miss my eldest son's wedding in New Orleans. My first child, my first son, was set to marry a beautiful young lady in New Orleans. I had to miss it. My wonderful husband had the wedding live-streamed to my hospital TV. Some dear friends missed the wedding and stayed with me in the room to watch the wedding with me. Now, two years later, my second son is getting married in March 2020, and I will attend.

Truly I feel like the luckiest girl in the world.

I'm here to share my story, to use my voice so others will keep the faith and believe in the power of prayers.

—Paula Simm

*For your reflection*: What is prayer to you? Is prayer important in your life?

*For his invisible attributes, namely his eternal power and divine nature, have been clearly perceived, ever since the creation of the world, in the things that have been made. —Romans 1:20*

## The Voice I Hear

Years ago when I heard others say, "I heard God speak to me," I felt anger and disappointment. My thinking long ago was, "He is not speaking to me." After attending silent retreats for twenty-one years, sitting in contemplative prayer, and truly connecting to Christ, I now am very familiar with God's voice. To be honest, it's never been an audible one for me.

God communicates with each of us in a very unique way. He connects with us in a way He knows we'll understand. The mystery is that He relates to all individuals, meeting us where we are when we are connected. For myself it's an intuitive experience, a knowing in my heart and in my body that leaves no doubt, yet no proof or evidence that it's Him. He alerts my body, and I listen from my heart. I've pondered the many ways that help me connect to hear His voice.

Sight. Many times a supernatural appearance that conveys an epiphany or revelation. Sunsets, rain, rainbows, feathers falling from the sky, sun rays surrounding me like arms wrapped around and holding me. God has given us spiritual eyes through which His divine truth enters my mind and heart. A knowing, some- thing beyond a shadow of a doubt, where my faith is not blind and my heart listens.

Animals. I sit and watch birds, cows, dogs, spiders, squirrels, and all God's creatures. They speak through their behavior and actions, pointing us to our common creator. They seem to see so clearly and simply. I take what I watch and learn from them every time I sit still.

Music. Good songs come from the heart and experiences. Songs can strike a chord within my heart that can bring me to joy and laughter; yet other music speaks to me, leading me to weep in sadness. In the Book of Psalms, David wrote many songs through his life experiences, and they have become prayers for us. In this way God's voice comes through the sound of music.

Art. This can express how we feel, and I believe art is designated by God as another form of worship and prayer. My collaging and writing are forms of art that take time and effort … a way of telling my stories. It has all become a huge part of my healing process from past traumas.

Nature. Saving the best for last, God longs to speak to us through his creation. The awe and wonder of watching waves on the beach, rain and snow falling, hiking or driving through mountains, or along a coastline—his whole universe. God longs to satisfy us in ways that bring us peace. We might not always understand or discern his message, but I've learned to let God speak in whatever way He desires, and it will be the voice I hear.

—Denise Broussard

*For your reflection*: Can you hear the loving voice of the Father by embracing mystery? Will you allow the Creator to speak to you in a way you will know and understand?

## Do Prayers Matter?

When I was first studying storytelling, I entered a contest in which tellers were asked to tell an entire story in 55 words or less. For a while, I imagined super-short stories about everyone I saw—in airports, in grocery stores, in restaurants. My world became filled with stories, whether they happened or not.

One day, on a flight to the West Coast, I was seated next to a young boy traveling alone. He later told me he was only ten. I forgot about story gathering while I spent a few hours listening to him. He had such a need to talk, and I had nowhere else I needed to go at 23,000 feet.

That night, I turned back into the short-storyteller, and wrote this:

*For Anthony,*

> *Alone on the plane, ten, messy blond hair, bright eyes, small scar on the cheek facing me.*

> *His Dad is in prison. Hates his Mom's pregnancy—won't say it.*

> *Lonely—can't say it.*

> *I let him win Crazy Eights. He laughs. Then I see the twelve-inch scar.*

> *I wonder if my prayers for him matter.*

I've since pondered that question from time to time. As years have passed, and as I have observed my own life and the lives of so many others, one thing has become clear to me:

Prayers always matter.

We may never see what effect they have, and it may be that the ones we pray for are never even aware a prayer has been said for them.

Nonetheless, I am sure it matters a great deal whenever prayers are said. Prayers help things change.

Anthony is now a young man somewhere. I still occasionally send up a prayer for him, pray he has kept his heart open in hard circumstances, pray he has found the comfort and companion-
ship he craved.

I will never know how it all played out, but I am sure my prayers did matter.

—Patricia Drury Sidman

*For your reflection:* From the place within you that is intentional and grounded, what is your prayer for today?

## The Locale of Prayer

In this time of Covid-19, I, like most of you, am investigating how I navigate the world; how I engage with others, with myself, and with all the mirrors that are flashed constantly through the media and by the way others are engaging now.

We are certainly being given mirrors across all choices of what we deem proper to absurd to dangerous. It is becoming beyond bizarre in my view. But it is all a mirror by which to make decisions about the way I think, behave, and believe, because I feed into this collective and give it strength or lessen its impact. I am part of the problem or I am part of the solution. Please God, help me be part of the solution!

I noticed something in my prayer this morning that I have probably noted before, maybe many times, but today it was so clear as to be grasped, and it carried authority: "Look at this, and really look at this." So I did.

This morning, as I was in prayer for the planet to assist healing the divisions and envisioning wholeness for us all, it came to me that my throat was tight and that I had a slight fear in my heart that was constricting my throat.

Absolutely, I believe we can and will benefit from prayer when we are in fear and distress. I also believe when I am praying for healing and envisioning wholeness I want to come from a place of love, calm, and peace in my heart.

I used the imagery of draining the fear from my throat and letting it wash away, pour out of my feet and fingers and, with deep breaths, I moved my attention into my heart and began to connect to the planet again, this time with much more love and peace.

I know some of us get tight in the belly or maybe our head feels like it is too full. I offer that you let those places soften and drain from your body; deep breaths help the process, smiling as you do it helps as well. Drain it all away and settle in your heart. Hold your intended healing focus in your heart and in your vision, however that looks for you—we all "see" differently.

—Avis Lyons LeBlanc

***For your reflection:*** Practice letting go of tension or anxiety through your breath, a smile, and release.

## Space

Making space for God,
giving voice to my needs,
giving voice to gratitude,
giving voice to praises,
entering into the mystery,
entering into love.

In that love space are the secrets of my life
deep hurts, fears, anxieties, anger confessed.
In that love space are my secret longings, yearnings, questions.
In that love space true self can come forward,
the whole of me, the essence of me.
In that love space I am held, comforted, and given strength.
In that love space I feel Mercy and Compassion cradling me.

It is a place of safety and refuge,
a nest of nurturing where faith grows,
a home for dreams and hopes.
It is a place of whispered words of love, and of love songs.

—Trudy Gomez

*For your reflection:* Allow yourself to enter a safe space, a place of
acceptance and love.

# Questions and Observations

Photo by Trudy Gomez

*It is what you are that heals, not what you know. —Carl Jung*

**Observations**

Like the earth
on tilted axis,
the universe leans
toward balancing
the scales.

Sometimes I need
not interfere,
but rather remain
a silent witness
to the moment.

It may be that
my only business
is to be a sentinel,
simply observing life
doing what it does,

taking no position
nor poison.
Refusing to drink of
the cup of judgement
full of itself.

Though it may
appear as such,
some things aren't
broken and not
in need of fixing.

Instead, I'll draw
a breath from
the common air

of humanity, trusting
that the universe

knows what is hidden
and exactly how to
right the wrongs.
Sometimes, ignorance
may be bliss

but arrogance
can be hell
when I think I know
and don't know
that I don't.

—Wendi Romero

*For your reflection:* May you simply observe life today.

## Paradox

Dragonflies dancing in the breeze
to the tunes of bird songs,
Bees gathering nectar and pollen from honeysuckle.
So, why this melancholy?

Waking from a lonely broken sleep,
walking through a quiet house,
Feelings of
loneliness
longing
missing

This morning I read a quote from PIR VILAYAT INAYAT KHAN:
"Don't be concerned about being disloyal to your pain by being joyous."

Does that apply to longing and missing?
When I stepped into sunshine,
when I saw the dancing dragonflies,
heard the bird songs,
my spirit lifted,
the loneliness, the longing intermingled with joy.

Can one know true joy without experiencing pain?
Can I give myself permission to settle into joy,
the joy of dancing butterflies, birdsong serenades.
Gathering sweet moments like bees gathering nectar?

Realizing, yes, grief can coexist with joy.

—Trudy Gomez

*For your reflection:* How do you live with the paradoxes of life?

## Things Happen

Today is March 17, 2020, and we are in an unprecedented battle with a virus, one that we knew nothing about mere months ago. I wonder what the look back will be when this is published.

Life can change with stunning rapidity. I will make it personal and name my little things: My pool is closed; my library is closed. I had to cancel a retreat I was giving. I grapple with myself as being in "the elderly high-risk group." My friends can't go see their lonely older relatives in the nursing home. My sportscaster son has no sports to report. You can fill in all the blanks for yourself. Crushing disappointment for some, economic disasters for others.

There are, no doubt, deep spiritual lessons in this situation. The first one is that we must expect change. Change is *the* constant of life. We get all our little ducks in a row and then some big cat comes along and swats them all out of line. It happens. It happens every day. Flexibility allows us to thrive.

A second lesson is that we are not in control. We can seek to control our thoughts, but that's about it. Greedily stockpiling groceries may give us a sense of control, but it's not real. It doesn't change the uncertainty of the future. It just takes goods from others who might need them. Having 20 cans of chicken and rice soup won't make us safer. (Although I did order some toilet paper from Amazon, just because I could.)

Things happen that we never expect and cannot control. I might have devised a different system, but that is the way it is. Rather than being shocked and affronted, we can say, "Okay, what now? How can I help?" I didn't expect the answer to be, "Stay home." I didn't expect the answer to be a question: "What does my life mean now?" It's a time to embrace the larger questions.

Don't think that I handle all this with the smile of a saint. I don't. I write about what I struggle with. But in the quiet now, I do have the time and space to be grateful for what I have and to be with what is.

You may be much like me. Your home is comfortable, and you have everything you need. We could count our blessings. It's an opportunity to do things we don't normally do. Meditate. Draw. Write poetry. Read. Finally get those papers organized. (Must I? Ha!) Write letters. Ponder and pray. My sister who lives near Shreveport says that they walk the school track each day, keeping six feet between people, but smiling and encouraging one another. I have been practicing sitting on my patio and just being. I have the opportunity to shed the bad habit of needing to be busy to feel good about myself.

As our isolation increases, this is a time to open the heart. To delve into spiritual practice. This is not a problem of the United States of America but of the whole world community. It's an opportunity to see that, in many ways, there are no borders. They are illusions. We are global and we share global problems.

And it's time to plant my caladiums. Right here at home.

—Lyn Holley Doucet

***For your reflection***: What was your experience of the coronavirus crisis? How did it increase your spirituality, if it did?

## Out of Place

Oh fallen, old, and out of place, you seem to reach out to be saved from the flowering beauty that imitates the Sun, which is alive and slowly engulfing your wood.

Your broken arms reach out, still.

But one notices you are motionless, but useful!

Oh, to be sat on in the midst of the beauty that imitates the Sun! And to be alive again to experience your worth!

—Cheryl Delahoussaye

*For your reflection*: Choose a picture/image and write about it.

*But they who wait for the Lord shall renew their strength; they shall mount up with wings like eagles, they shall run and not be weary; they shall walk and not faint. —Isaiah 40:31*

**Waiting**

Early morning rush,
getting stuck waiting
in bumper-to-bumper traffic
on the Basin Bridge.

Waiting is the hardest thing to do.
Sometimes patiently, sometimes not.
Calm waiting, frantic waiting.
I have experienced them all.

Waiting to catch a glimpse of a sunrise.
Waiting for those gorgeous sunsets.
Then wait some more to celebrate
the moon and bright stars.

With caregiving, bringing loved ones
to doctor appointments to sit
in a waiting room.

Sitting in a hospital emergency area,
waiting for an examining room,
for a doctor to arrive.

Praying and waiting patiently
for diagnoses, X-rays, blood work,
or other tests for family or friends.

Praying and waiting for updates
when someone is in surgery,
while waiting on God's response.
It's fun to hurry to a concert

to get that great seat, only to wait
for the curtain to rise
for the show to begin.

How about waiting
for your seat at a restaurant?
Then wait for that fabulous meal
to be prepared and served.

Waiting is the hardest thing to do.
We literally do it every day.
Waiting, I've come to realize

is another grace given to us.
We just need to shift the way
we think about it.

Our Lord patiently waits
for us to return to him.
Just as the father waited
for his prodigal son.

God's patient waiting
continues to show me
just how much he loves me.

Waiting for traffic to move,
I am gathering strength;
preparing my heart,

my mind, my body,
for what's to come.
I wait with my Lord
with a grateful heart.

Eyes wide open
to see His beauty
surrounding me—

a knowing in my heart
that He loves me
and believes in me
in the waiting.

—Denise Broussard

*For your reflection*: In your daily lives, how will you begin to handle all the different ways we wait? Can we be still before the Lord and wait patiently with Him seeing this as a season of preparation instead?

## The Most Powerful Question I Was Ever Asked

Every so often I come upon a question that makes me think. Most people do. I may find it in an essay, a speech, a sermon, even a book or a movie.

Once, however, years ago, I was asked a stop-dead-in-your-tracks question that changed my life. If you are lucky, you will someday be asked one of those.

I went to a personal development workshop, and we had just completed an exercise designed to give us insight into our leadership skills, relationship to authority, and capacity for vision. It was a sneaky little exercise that set each of us up to inadvertently reveal some truths about ourselves. I won't give any more details so if you ever encounter it, you will be open to its full impact.

It was an ego-smashing exercise, to say the least. I don't think anyone who participated was especially happy with the self-awareness that came from it. I was frankly horrified to see my fears and my compensating behaviors so brilliantly exposed. Then, with all our egos shaken and vulnerable, and all our hearts unusually open, the leader asked *the question*.

It was this: "What do you stand for that isn't about you?"

Years later, I am still working with that question. First I thought, *What if there isn't anything?* Then I tried some obvious answers—words found in the language of my values and dreams. But those were still about me. There were platitudes about my work: me, again. There were my opinions, my spirituality, my politics—still me.

It was only after I thought about a few famous people who did seem to stand for something that wasn't about them that I came to understand where to look for answers. Those I could think of did so at great cost to their health, wealth, security, and even life, people like Mahatma Gandhi, Mother Teresa, Martin Luther King, Jr. These people changed the world.

But there are others without names or fame. Heroic first responders who run toward the fire or gunshots to save others. People who collect cans of food and distribute them to others who lack enough food. People who regularly donate their blood, not knowing who will eventually receive it. People who hold the door for someone struggling with a walker. They also change the world.

Walking with that question for decades now has changed me. It led to me to change my work and re-orient many of my values and perceptions. I have come to know that question as a great gift. It still helps me direct myself and see what steps I am called to take next. May the question bring you the richness it has brought me.

—Patricia Drury Sidman

*For your reflection:* What do *you* stand for that isn't about you?

*At a writer's retreat we were given a jumping-off point to write from:
Dear Monk I know why you want to sit on Cold Mountain ...*

## Dear Monk

I've learned that quiet and solitude can be lonely at times.
I long for the Missed One; the one whom I knew was out and about, near,
the one who would lie beside me at night.

I am learning more and more that being alone and loneliness share
common roots but mean different things.

There are times when I am sick of my own company and seek out
companionship, background noise, anything to distract from the
loneliness.

I am learning to be on my own.
I am learning that too much togetherness can be just
as lonely as being alone,
that there are times I need to have my head in the clouds, to lie under a
tree, to watch, to listen to the birds sing, the breeze whisper through the
leaves, to the quiet.

So, Dear Monk, I know why you want to sit on Cold Mountain.
It is a place to observe
Not just the things around me, but to observe me.
To glimpse at the one learning to navigate,
To learn how I am being transformed into the Who I am
at this moment.
To contemplate the question, Am I changing or was this already me?

—Trudy Gomez

*For your reflection*: Sit with yourself and contemplate, *Dear Monk I
know why you want to sit on Cold Mountain ...* Where does this lead
you? Write about it.

# Quiet and Contemplation

Photo by Wendi Romero

*The trouble is you think you have time. —Buddha*

## Don't Leave Too Soon

The breeze blows
rustling the leaves,
the swing sways
moving me like
a pendulum, to and fro.
I hear an inner voice say,
"don't leave too soon."

Listen to what
your soul has to say.
Hear the song of the birds,
watch the cows lazily roam,
see the moss dance over
the sleeping graves—
"don't leave too soon."

I sit where I once sat
long before I knew
what I know now.
Another old friend just died
and the years are turning on
themselves like a bale of hay—
"don't leave too soon."

Time is winding
tighter and tighter.
I've lived longer than
the days remaining.
I sit to ponder that alone,
and don't leave
a minute too soon.

—Wendi Romero

***For your reflection***: Remember that you hold only a given amount of
time in your hands.

*So shall my word be that goes forth from my mouth. It shall not return to me void, but shall do my will, achieving the end for which I sent it.*
*—Isaiah 55:11*

## Hello Sadness, What Have You Come to Tell Me?

Raindrops fall slowly to the earth, one at a time.
I hear them. I can almost count them.
Each following the direction of Creator.
Heaviness is all around me, it fills me up.
Sadness, what have you come to tell me?

Sadness says, "Be in me for I have been sent for change."
Just as rain is needed to nourish the grass, plants, trees,
I am an element that can lead to transformation
following the intention of our Lord.

This shadow has its own purpose.
It is a remembering from deep inside of who you are called to be.
Your deepest self is summoning a shift.
The nature of your being has its own unique purpose.

Let Spirit guide you each step of the way.
Do not be led by the ways in which others are led.
Theirs is a different way;
not more, not less, but different.

Let the quiet seep into your very core.
Listen for Me; be in me.
In this shadow there is light where hope rises, making a way for joy to come.

For even as the raindrops fall to the earth
trust in Me that my word will be done in you.

—Velma LeBlanc Cheramie

*For your reflection*: When sadness comes, spend time in silence, asking
God what is being asked of you today.

*The Lord said, Go out and stand on the mountain in the presence of the Lord, for the Lord is about to pass by.* —*1 Kings 19:11*

**Escape the Noise**

It is in the stillness we can hear
God's gentle whisper in our hearts.
It comes so quietly
as those snowflakes I watch
falling each morning.

Telluride, Colorado.
Breathtakingly beautiful views,
daily experiences of silence.
A wonderful opportunity
to calm down,
a place to tune out—
to escape the noise.

Watching the sunrise,
I see melting icicles
right outside my window.
They slowly drip to the
snow-covered ground.

Love the daily gondola rides.
More silence experienced,
but my heart is heavy witnessing
so many hopping on and immediately
grabbing cell phones.

Consumed with staring at a screen,
instead of God's creation …
beautiful landscapes and majestic
mountains, sun-rays streaming
through the trees, and snow
falling, covering all things.
We take so much for granted.

My family and I gather
after long days on the slopes.
We are certainly guaranteed
extra noise and celebration.
So many conversations going on
at the same time as we prepare
to cook and enjoy our delicious
meals and evening cocktails.
All saying our blessings, thanking God
for our food, family, friends—our trip.

At the end of each day
games are played
in front of the fireplace,
Drinking hot cocoa
with lots of marshmallows.
A lot of laughter, sharing the day's
events with sweet expressions of love.
My heart, my cup overflows.

I am filled with joy …
not allowing too much noise
to overwhelm me.
The beauty in all this—
when I sit quietly in between
those active noisy times, I find
my solo time with my Lord
to be even sweeter.

For I know, I believe, I trust.
God has allowed all of this to happen.
For that, I am very grateful.

—Denise Broussard

*For your reflection*: Can we truly quiet our hearts through the busyness
and noise of the world?

*Snow absorbs sound. When it's snowing there's plenty of space between snowflakes, meaning that there is also less space for sound waves to bounce around. The world really does slow down when it snows.*

## Slowing Down

Anxious is the feeling I felt before I departed on a long-awaited trip to Colorado with my children and grand-daughters. I was leaving behind my responsibility of caregiving with the uncertainty of loved ones suffering with major health issues. I repeated to myself, "I am not in control, but I know who is." I was forced to "let go and let God" once again. It brought back a memory of when I attended one of my silent retreats. The first night, the priest strongly suggested for everyone to leave cell phones in their cars. He wanted us to trust that we were where we were supposed to be and that God would take care of our families while we were away. Sometimes it's easier said than done. If we continue to say we trust and believe, then we must stand by what we say and surrender all to our Father. He will ease our hearts and minds, reminding us that He is in control, not us.

Many arrangements were made before I left, and I had to trust God's plan—that all would be taken care of according to His word. "Do not be anxious, but in prayer and petitions, with thanksgiving, present your request to God, and the peace which transcends all understanding will guard your heart and mind in Christ Jesus" (Philippians 4:6-7). I took care of what I could with the hospital, doctors, home health, and personal care assistants, then let God handle the rest. Even dealing with many issues by phone for a couple of days from Colorado, I slowly allowed myself to enjoy the time away, and it all ended up well.

This gift of slowing down, not needing to hurry, taking time to listen, and seeing God's gifts is what the Great Physician ordered for my anxious and worried mind. Let's think about what we do. Most times, we worry and fear about something that has not even happened and actually might not ever. We say to ourselves and to others, "But what if?" There is a lot of energy wasted on worry and fear, when it just might not come to be. I think of Matthew 8:26, when Jesus said, "Ye of little faith, why are you so afraid?" I admit, I'm human and this verse sometimes describes me as a doubter of God's abilities, as well as the abilities of others.

In the early Colorado mornings, I'm gifted with no sound, silence, and stillness, as I watch snow fall right outside my window. I gaze at the trees decorated with white lights and the snow-covered ground shining like diamonds as the sun rises. It is truly a winter wonderland. It's calm and serene ... exactly what our hearts crave and starve for at times. It doesn't have to be found on the mountain, but wherever your own heart desires.

Before long, I hear little girls' giggles and words of disbelief at something they've never witnessed before—the gift of snow. There is beauty in watching the snow falling quietly, and in the way that no one here seems to move too fast. There is a slow pace with no one in a hurry, an attitude that all of us should take note of. We, who live in the city are always rushed and over- whelmed by busyness, but a fast pace doesn't always serve us well.

God's beauty in creation is all over the world, even in your own backyard—for us to enjoy, to live in awe of, to love in mystery. No matter where we are, the Holy Spirit wants us to slow down, not feel guilty, and just smell the coffee.

—Denise Broussard

*For your reflection*: How can we slow down and quiet our hearts in the sometimes foolish pace we allow to happen in our daily lives?

## Welcoming the Quiet

Today is a dreary Monday in almost the middle of Fall. Now, my house, quiet most mornings.

Having arrived at middle age, I've learned to embrace this stillness and the freedom to journal. The last few weeks however, I've found it hard to write. I've been going inward to try and discover why.

Maybe there is no real answer. I know that sometimes when I welcome the quiet, other thoughts and emotions rise to the surface. Without giving in to distraction, I gently breathe in presence.

I am continuing to serve my inner self. To serve the old and new wounds. To navigate toward wholeness—and I'm grateful for how far I've come. Each life event has brought me here to this day.

—Gina Bradley

*For your reflection:* Sit in solitude with a pen and your journal. What are the writings of your heart?

*From a writing exercise with the prompt: When the world is quiet …*

**When the World Is Quiet**

That gradual awakening that takes place
When the world is quiet
Soft stirrings
Gradual illumination
Edges
Outlines
Shapes
Slowly taking form

Have I really emerged from my deep underworld
Do vestiges of the past still cling to me
Have I shed those things as I move toward the light
Do I carry the stink of the graves I have dug for myself
Am I a walking corpse
Am I the ghost-woman
Am I resurrected, reborn

Shake off the darkness, shed the ties of the past
Make peace with what came before
Past is past, let go, don't hold on
Move on, move forward
Be the new being
Be the new creation
Be the resurrected woman.

—Trudy Gomez

***For your reflection***: Journal using the prompt "When the world is
quiet …" and explore where your thoughts and feelings lead.

# Seasons and Changes

Photo by Michelle Lafleur MacFadyen

## When You Say

When you say *the night air*, I am in it. It smells still.
I am young again. My body is light. It loves without

knowing what love is yet. When you say *night air*,
I am standing at my bedroom window. It still has

the night's dust lying quietly on its sill. The window's
thin screen smells like time passing and so much time

has passed through; I am not as young when you say
*night air* the next time. Now, night crickets begin

to sing. I pull the covers up under my chin, wait for
you to rest next to me as if we were young again and

the night air was never for sleeping. It was the entrance
for each other, to enter each other as the night air lifted

into perfume and whatever was possible became so high
the wind wanted to be near us. We said, Come in,

we were already waiting for your caress in the midst
of the night air.

—Sidney Creaghan

***For your reflection***: Do you remember when we used to sleep with the
windows open and the night air would enter our rooms and the night
sounds in turn would enter on the air? Take a moment to contemplate
that time and if you choose, write about our open-windowed world
compared to our closed window air-conditioned world. Has it aided in
removing us from the natural world? Are we safer now?

# The Gift of Places

All the places and spaces in my life are gifts.
My neighborhood whose sidewalks were gravel roads,
connected me to friends, school, church, and my father's store.

Songs on the porch swing as we sang my youngest sister
to sleep, so we could go play in the yard,
created a closeness in our family.

The skating rink with the colored lights and music, opened up a world of
imagination and possibility. Gaining the skill to skate backwards was a
great achievement, and pop-the-whip was exhilarating.

Sitting on the back porch of the rectory, I was taught the basics of
Gregorian chant. The beauty of chant was an introduction to melody and
worship, and the distinction between performance and praise.

Working in our family's store gave me an insight into family finances.
I was aware of how much money it took to keep us clothed, fed, and
paying our bills; being a clerk developed skills of customer relations.

My father's trust in us was created by not giving us a salary
but saying to us, "Take whatever you need out of the cash register."

The lessons I learned in these experiences are pictures of love, security,
and adventure. They gave me strength to venture forth in life.

Remembering who I am in these places and spaces expands my heart,
feeding the flame of love and awakening me to who I am called to be.

—Betty Landreneau

*For your reflection:* What are the significant places in life that gave rise
to fear, joy, or courage?

*In every adult there's an eternal child, something that is always becoming.*
*That is the part that continually wants to develop and become whole.*
—*Carl Jung*

## All the Ages

Something deep called
out to me from
"all the ages

I've ever been."
My feet hesitate
but my heart has

already crossed the line
back in time.
I see what used to be,

tall and wide,
still standing
in front of me.

Like rings of time
spiraled around a tree,
I've grown around

the child inside of me.
No borders between
my becoming

as one year passed into
the next. The trunk still
stands sturdy and sure.

While aged bent branches
sweep close to the ground,
others are still reaching

for the sky. I'm walking
through "all the ages
I've ever been."

—Wendi Romero

\*quote from Madcleine L'Engle

***For your reflection:*** Dare to discover your eternal child within.

*Happy the people who know you, Lord, who walk in the radiance of your face. —Psalm 89:16*

## Walking the Sands of Time

I walk along the shore of my life, hand in hand with my Lord against the winds of trouble and sorrow.

Sand sifting through my toes, sloughing away dried, dead cells just as your blood washed away my sins of yesterday.
Wind blowing indecision and fear behind me as my Lord
leads me forward into the light of the future.

He carries me in my weakness.
He leads me as I look toward Him.
The winds of change blow over me as I lean forward.
He steadies me in the gusts, always faithful.

In you alone, O Lord, can I trust!
You are my Rock, my salvation, my only hope.
Lead me, guide me, carry me, O Lord, across the sands of my time here on this earth.
Your will be done in me, that I may be with you in Eternity. Amen.

—Velma LeBlanc Cheramie

*For your reflection*: The seasons of our lives change over the years. What is the "theme" of your life at this moment? What is the compass that guides you?

## Hibernation

In these gray, cold, rainy days of winter it is hard to think of anything
that energizes.
The dampness penetrates my very bones.
All I want to do is cocoon in my quilts and blankets with a cup of tea or
a bowl of soup.
I look at the things I need to do around the house,
Like taking down Christmas décor and think, eh
and then
just nap
mindlessly watch tv
read trashy books.
I take long steamy baths with the water halfway up the tub
I loll there until the hot water runs out
then back into sweats and wrapped up in blankets.
I dream of lying on a beach with the sun shining, me sinking into the
warm sand.
I reminisce about eating oatmeal in hot tubs as snow drifts down.
I long for a warm massage table with me draped in hot towels
slathered with fragrant oils turning my muscles to jelly.
My thoughts turn to saunas where warmth engulfs me.
Then I am reminded that earth is cocooning, hibernating, resting, being
restored.
Maybe that is what I am doing
I am returning to an atavistic form,
tapping into the ancient parts of me;
the one imprinted in DNA,
the one that lived in synergy with the seasons.
But mostly I think fuck winter.

—Trudy Gomez

*For your reflection:* How do you hibernate?

*When writing Haiku, I am in the moment. I guess that is true of all writing.*

**Haiku to the Seasons**

Winter. Inwardly
resting, waiting, breath deepens.
Anticipating.

Spring. Resurrection.
Greening concealed, overflows.
Abundantly lush.

Summer and fire.
Energetic and lively!
So is the harvest.

Indian Summer.
Last of the fruits and berries.
Birds are fattening.

Fall. Releasing to
lie dormant. Garden put to bed.
Grandeur on display!

—Avis Lyons LeBlanc

***For your reflection***: This might be a practice you find silence and presence in. I do 5, 7, 5 syllables to describe an entire experience.

*The great thing about getting older is that you don't lose all the other ages you've been. —Madeleine L'Engle*

## A Basket of Strawberry Reflections

My mother nudges me to get out of bed. It is barely dawn and time to head to the strawberry fields. It is a crisp, very early spring morning with the sun on the horizon. There is still a chill in the air as it brushes across my face. I wear a sweater to keep me warm until the sun rises. Dew remains on the ground causing my shoes to become damp, adding to my discomfort. My brothers and sisters are with me along with the seasonal help who came to live on the farm to help pick the strawberries. Mom starts out in the field with us until there are enough strawberries to begin sorting and packing to take to the distributors. It's not all work because my brothers like to add to the challenge of seeing who can pick the most berries.

Most all of the strawberry plants are very healthy with lots of growth on them. Great care was taken in the tilling of the soil, the planting, and finally surrounding the plants with pine needles to prevent the weeds from growing amongst the plants. That was one of my favorite duties. The pine needles are dropped on top of the plants. It is like searching for the plants when we create a little hole to pull the plants through and secure the pine needles tightly around them. Because the plants are nurtured so carefully, there were very few weeds and very few plants that look weak.

As I reflected on this memory, I was amazed to see someone in the field with us whom I never realized was present at the time. Jesus was watching us. He was pleased to see the love and attention that had gone into producing the strawberries. ("The seed that fell on rich soil, they are the ones, who when they have heard the word, embrace it with a generous and good heart and bear fruit through perseverance" Mk 4:20.) What a wonderful metaphor for life as it unfolds!

There was my family together, persevering with your love to produce the fruits of our labor. Little did I notice at the time the deeper meaning of harvesting love that was bigger than the strawberry field. Jesus was encouraging me to stay on the journey as I reflected. The rich soil of His love was and is present. Harvest times are seasonal, we prepare for them, work through them, and then rest. With His love, I recognize the seasons and allow the transformation to happen.

—Pat Low

*For your reflection*: When have you failed to see God's presence but recognized it later?

# Story and Meaning

Photo by Michelle Lafleur MacFadyen

*Love is a place of vulnerability. And yet, we are created to love one another.* —*Vicki Schmidt*

## Dad and Me

As a child, I knew when my dad-surgeon walked in the door at home: the pungent aroma of antiseptic and disinfectant announced his arrival. Did he fix a broken arm today? Did he get to pull a bullet out of someone's gut? Did he save a life today?

Dad didn't tell us of his daily battles against death in the OR. We learned from his silent cues. If he exiled himself to the bedroom without supper, he had lost the battle (a rare but impressionable occurrence). If we heard him making calls that night to check in, then we knew he was victorious; someone was going to make it through.

When I was in third grade, he came to speak to my class. All my friends held their hands high to ask questions. What makes you cough? Why do we get the hiccups? Will your insides stick together if you swallow your gum? He knew all the answers! And even gave one of my lucky friends a shiny new First Aid Kit. I smiled all day that day.

These days, I accompany Dad to the medical appointments for his own health challenges. It's time for other doctors to have the answers. I'm just there to help Dad remember what the answers are. I know it must be frustrating for him because he was once in command of the medical team—*he* was the fixer, the rescuer, the healer. And now he is forced to let go and depend on others to do the work.

Is that why I find Dad outside in his garden? Caring for plants, nurturing hot peppers to their spiciest potential and tending to the delicate white blooms on his rose bushes complete his day.

And yet, I have a feeling he is not fully content with this work.

Now that our roles are slowly starting to change—the child needing to parent and the caregiver needing care—how do we make this dance work so that we aren't stepping on each other's toes? How do I respect the dignity of my father? Is it by not running to the rescue? How do I show Dad more than anything that he is loved and appreciated for who he is and not just for what he used to do?

Dad faced many challenges as a practicing physician. He has new challenges now, and so do I. He taught me how to recover from setbacks and how to stay in the battle. He taught me that our lives are precious.

—Michelle Lafleur MacFadyen

*For your reflection:* How can you connect with an aging parent, neighbor, or friend, and express dignity and respect?

## Recipe or Re-creation?

My husband has a new obsession: night-time wild hog hunting. I think there will be a reality show on cable this fall all about this activity; thankfully he will not be one of the stars, although he is beginning to remind me of Drum Eaton, the bird-shooting character in *Steel Magnolias.*

As with some other rotating obsessions, armadillo killin' and raccoon trappin,' he belongs to a not-so-exclusive brotherhood of hog hunters (hog huntin').

He and his hunting buddy go out and bait said hogs about every other day with foodstuff donated by folks. They give them rice, molasses or old bread in hopes that they, the Intrepid Hunters, will kill a fatted pig. The hunters have set up a stand, a feeding station, and a camera to record the comings and goings of feral hogs. The hunting area is near Palmetto State Park and is overrun with hogs gone wild. At least the obsession provides food for the table; in fact we have run out of freezer space so hunter has gone out and procured another freezer. Enough already!

After one of his early kills, someone told him that they used the back bone of the hog to make a spaghetti sauce. That sparked the idea to try to recreate a dish I ate in Lucca, Italy: wild boar stew, a tomato based ragout.

I "googled" wild boar stew, and of course up came several recipes. Basically they had the same ingredients. I combined the recipes and went to work. I chopped (actually I confess to using the food processor) veggies, seasoned and browned pig, peeled tomatoes from the garden, and put everything in a big pot and poured in a bottle less one glass of red wine and set it to simmer.

It took hours for the meat to become tender and begin to fall off of the bones; wild porkers are tough! I then scooped meat and bones out of the gravy and shredded the meat like you would when making pulled pork. I used the immersion blender to smooth out the veggies in the gravy and let it simmer more to reduce. Did they use an immersion blender in the little Lucchesian trattoria? It is the 21st century, so one never knows.

When we finally sat down to eat, I was pretty pleased with the results, but the dish didn't quite live up to the one I savored in Italy. There was just a little something missing. Was it what the hog fed on? The wine? The herbs and spices? The tomatoes?

Was I just using a recipe to recreate a dish, or was I trying to recreate a memory—of sitting at little table outside of Trattoria da Leo on a cool May evening, drinking a great house red wine in tumblers served by the personable, zany waiter with the too-obvious name of Mario, who ran through the tables encouraging *bere più vino*, drink more wine!

Oh well, all I can say is, la dolce vita!

—Trudy Gomez

*For your reflection:* Food can evoke memories. What food evokes for you a fond memory?

*Home is where our story begins. —Annie Danielson*


## Windmills and Far Horizons

On our way home to Louisiana from Taos, NM a few years ago we
passed through the area where I spent my early years: Clayton, Sudan,
Texline, and home—Dalhart, Texas.

The grasslands through that area go on forever, as far as the eye can see
in all directions. There are probably some houses out there but none are
visible from the road. A very black, blacktop road, with a bright yellow
stripe in the middle, that winds like a ribbon going on and on. Fences
stretch along both sides of this black road and an occasional holding pen
for when it's cattle drive time. They have some really big cattle drives in
that vast country of huge ranches.

We stopped at a cafe in Des Moines, NM that was very good. We had
been there before and knew they had really good New Mexico food. Des
Moines, just as the few other towns we passed through, looked as though
they were lost in time. The people were like I remember people from my
youth. "Howdy, how you doin' today?"

It is bleak country, but a beauty lies within that bleakness. Maybe I
appreciate it less because I lived there, lived with the dry and the heat
and the extreme cold in winter with wind through it all. Wind blowing
almost constantly. Everything from a slight breeze all the way to a blow-
you-off-your-feet wind. It's probably why I don't like windy days now;
they wore me down.

Windmills standing against a backdrop of blue sky are enchanting for
me. Such peace and beauty when I see them, alone and … waiting. I
remember the tin cup that hangs on all windmill pumps and the metallic
taste when you fill it with the cold, clear water that comes from deep in
the earth. The clang, clang of the pipe in and out to pump the water is
a sound from my childhood that has a home-ness about it and a sound I
still love.

I was returning to my childhood on that particular blue-sky, puffy-white-cloud and sunny day as we drove along the black ribbon with miles of fenced range. Sometimes we would see a broken down old home that once held a family but now had been repurposed to hold tack and feed, no longer a place for eating, warming oneself, or finding comfort after a long day. Those old houses are all over that part of the country. We had one at a farm of ours. I always felt the loneliness of those houses, like someone's dreams were in ruins. Of course they might have moved up and out, it just never felt that way with those old houses. There is something about porches falling down that seems so lonely to me. I can see my granddad sitting in his rocking chair on a porch just like those used to be, and I loved to see him there. His porch is gone too.

The skies are magnificent, like Montana, a big sky. You have blue, blue sky as the dome above, and it reaches all the way to the ground, nothing to break the view. The grassland is true "earth tones" in their pale greens, muted tans, yellows, and palest of orange. It is truly a striking landscape. I suppose if one didn't know the country they might not have that love/hate relationship that I experience when I travel through there. I love the nostalgia and the grandeur of the vast country but I dislike the extremes of the weather and the harshness of the climate and only an occasional scrub tree in view.

A rain shower—well, actually a rain spatter—came along. There was no visible sign that the rain had come but the smell was wonderful. Fragrance of rabbit sage and dry earth blended with scanty splashes of rain and clumps of grass, creating the raw perfume of nature. Freshness of rain on dry earth: heartwarming, recollecting, sensory remembering. I have driven between Albuquerque and Tucumcari when the Saguaro were in bloom. Fields of them standing with blooms covering their arms and legs. The prickly pear were blooming profusely too. It was incredible. Not just a plant here and there but miles of them, brilliant pink and yellow among the pale colors of grey-green and brown against the dazzling blue sky.

I spent my childhood in that country, going about my childhood days. Some were spent with Daddy on our farms, drinking from the tin cup, hearing the windmill clang, clang and working with him out in that dry, seemingly uncompromising land. He always loved the land. He would stop to look at the beauty around him and point to a clump of sunflowers or the cows grazing against a backdrop of blue sky and puffy clouds and the horizon as far as we could see. He always seemed to have his eye on the horizon. Was there a dream there? It seemed there was nowhere on earth he would rather be.

—Avis Lyons LeBlanc

*For your reflection:* Is there an image, a scent, or other sensory memory that holds home-ness for you? Do you allow yourself go there?

*When we know about our ancestors, when we sense them as living and as supporting us, then we feel connected to the genetic life-stream, and we draw strength and nourishment from this. —Philip Carr-Gomm*

## My Story

My grandmother was a Jewish flapper. She was courageous, adventurous, and smart. She defied authority and lived by her own rules, and I loved her dearly.

She immigrated to America from Romania at the age of eight. She told the story of coming over on a boat, by herself, to meet her sister who was living in St. Louis. She was leaning over the ship's rail and came close to falling overboard before being saved by fellow passengers. Her adventurous spirit was evident even at this early age.

As a young woman, she made her way to New Orleans with her girlfriend and stayed there until the day she died. The details leading up to this adventure were never shared with me, but she made the most of living in the Big Easy.

She was always self-sufficient. Even though she married my grandfather and bore my father, her sense of adventure never left. She refused to stay locked into a conventional marriage with my alcoholic grandfather and divorced him early on. My father reported that she was the first person in Orleans parish to receive both alimony and child support.

She went on to work at The Roosevelt Hotel and an upscale perfume store on Royal Street. It may not be coincidental that, between professions, I sold perfume at upscale retail establishments as well.

According to legend she had many male suitors, all Jewish of course, who wanted to marry her but she refused. She remained single until the end of her life. She eventually moved into an exclusive long-term care facility owned and operated by the New Orleans Jewish Foundation. There she resided among the affluent members of New Orleans society even becoming Mardi Gras Queen one year.

By all accounts, I am very much her granddaughter. I resemble her in many ways both physically and characteristically. I too am adventurous, courageous, and willing to defy authority. This freedom seeking independence has been both a blessing and a curse. It has allowed me to achieve lofty goals even though I had my share of bumps and bruises along the way. I don't take NO for an answer very easily and refuse to be controlled by anyone.

I did manage to stay married much longer than she did, forty-two years to be exact, but always remained independent. As a widow and single woman now, I feel her energy all around me. She comes to me in spirit when I am facing a tough decision or required action, and she propels me to move forward without fear. I call on her frequently and ask for inspiration and guidance and—believe it or not—I receive it!

I am now a grandmother to a beautiful baby girl, and I find myself guiding her in the ways of the world. She too is showing a feisty spirit and dominant personality, which is in the genes. She recently learned how to walk in high heels! My grandmother would be so proud!!

—Linda Jacobs Gondron

*For your reflection:* Do you have a cherished ancestor to call on for their inspiration and guidance?

*O, Mary of Magdala, help me to love and serve Jesus as you did. Give me your strength and inner wisdom to love in bold gestures. Amen.*

## Mary Magdalene

In January, 2020, Our Lady of Fatima Church in Lafayette, LA was blessed to receive a tour of the Relics of St. Mary Magdalene from her Basilica of Sainte Baume in Southern France.

Father Racine, Rector of the Basilica, stated that over the centuries, Mary of Magdala has taken on the roles of many references of women in the Bible. When Jesus looked upon her as the sinful woman, she received his gaze of Divine Mercy, which moved her to tears. As she knelt at his feet, she bathed them with her tears, kissed and anointed them with nard, and wiped them with her hair. This sinful woman gave Him the best she had to give, without words, by her bold gesture of honor, love, adoration, and gratitude for the love He gave to her. She repented for her sins because Mercy gazed upon her.

As Mary, sister of Martha, she sat at the feet of Jesus to be fed by His Word. She adored Him. She chose to receive everything He had to give and to serve Him, as opposed to serving others.
According to Jesus, she chose the better.

Mary wept at the foot of the cross and stayed with Him until the end, next to His Mother and the apostle, John. She loved Jesus deeply and was loved greatly by Him. He appeared to her when she was the first at the tomb. She thought He was the gardener, but when He called her name, she recognized Him, responding with "Rabboni," which means "Teacher." Like us, when we look at the Eucharist, physically we see bread; but, when Jesus calls our name, we finally recognize Him as the Body, Blood, Soul, and Divinity of the Christ.

Fr. Racine also stated, after the death of Jesus, many of his followers were killed or banished from the land. Legend is that Mary of Magdala, Lazarus, Mary Salome, Martha, and several others were loaded on a boat and set out to sea without oars, sails, or food. They remained afloat, almost perishing in a storm, but eventually landed in southern France. Mary of Magdala ended up in the Sainte Baume region, where she was given the opportunity to take the love of Jesus to others, to preach His Words, to teach what He taught her. She preached to them that instead of offering animal sacrifices to God, we are to offer our very own lives to God as our sacrifice. Our bodies are our alabaster jar, and our lives are our very perfume that we offer to Jesus in thanksgiving for the gift of salvation that He gave us.

Personally, I marvel at the depth of her love for Jesus and His Word. I believe that she understood the heart of Jesus. She knew Him. She recognized Him. She understood exactly what Jesus was trying to teach them, so she was able to speak His Word to the apostles at a deeper level. But sorrowfully, they did not understand where she was coming from.

I am in awe of the boldness of Mary Magdalene, walking into a room full of men, uninvited, with an alabaster jar of expensive nard, falling at the feet of Jesus, bathing them with her tears of anointing, and wiping them with her long hair. I can only imagine the shock and disdain of these men toward her insolence in entering their space to perform this act. When Jesus saw the reaction of Simon the Pharisee, who had invited Him, He said to him, *"Do you see this woman? When I entered your house, you did not give me water for my feet, but she has bathed them with her tears and wiped them with her hair. You did not give me a kiss, but she has not ceased kissing my feet since the time I entered. You did not anoint my head with oil, but she anointed my feet with ointment. So, I tell you, her many sins have been forgiven; hence, she has shown great love. But the one to whom little is forgiven, loves little."* Luke 7:44-47

Judas Iscariot indignantly complained that this oil, worth someone's annual salary, could have been sold and given to the poor instead of being poured out over Jesus, causing the others to become infuriated with her. Jesus said, *"Let her alone. Why do you make trouble for her? She has done a good thing for me. The poor you will always have with you, and whenever you wish you can do good to them, but you will not always have me. She has done what she could. She has anticipated anointing my body for burial. Amen, I say to you, wherever the gospel is proclaimed to the whole world, what she has done will be told in memory of her."* Mark 14:6-9

How many times have I withheld a word or action out of fear and trepidation that it would be inappropriate, cause judgment about me, or simply because it would just not be enough? Sadly, I must admit, too many times. Jesus said about Mary Magdalene, "She has done what she could." Wow! Such a simple statement that means so much! I want to do what I can to encourage, love and help someone, no matter how small it is, no matter how I might be judged by others. It is truly the least I can do as I move forward in my life. I pray for the boldness in love that Mary Magdalen lived in her own way on this earth. Proselytizing was not her way, but living and giving from deep within the strength of her love; and trusting that it would be enough. This I can relate to and this I aspire to, in Jesus' Name. Amen.

—Velma LeBlanc Cheramie

*For your reflection*: Can you recall a time when you held back the love you felt because you feared being judged? Consider writing your story.

*Story is a medicine which strengthens and arights the individual and the community. —Clarissa Pinkola Estes*

## It's Time for the Medicine of Story

Hear the whisper of Spirit,
"Come to the circle
where solace abides."
Find clarity,
community,
shelter.

Story circles,
spirals.
Listen, speak,
hear, reveal.
Embrace
the container
where kin
are recognized.

Weave your thread
with others
into the dazzling
tapestry
that reveals—

all is one.

—Avis Lyons LeBlanc

***For your reflection***: Your willingness to participate fully in a circle might give those who are more timid permission to add their vibrant thread to the tapestry.

*The sacred plot of my life—the main narrative strand.*

## The Roar Within

A passion for honoring my dignity and yours
acceptance and encouraging love
embodying life-giving spirit
tending the blossoming soul

Acceptance and encouraging love
pondering impoverishing attitudes of self righteousness
tending the blossoming soul
patient hopeful trust

Pondering impoverishing attitudes of self righteousness
embodying life-giving spirit
patient hopeful trust
a passion for honoring my dignity and yours

—Elsa Diana Mendoza

*For your reflection*: What roars within the depths of your spirit?

# The Spirit and the Power

Photo by Denise Broussard

## Notice, Listen

Accidentally locked outside in the late dawn of morning
I sit and look around at the things neglected,
the things I HAVE to do;
the things that cause my belly to be tied up in knots.

Rising sun calls, look up, stretch, reach, notice!
Pink-lit clouds give way to blue sky as sun rises above treetops
all is painted with a rosy golden glow.
I see color now instead of shades of gray.

I look among the trees and see light filter through and into woods
I try to capture it with memory and camera,
but it shifts and changes and flees to another place, against another leaf,
a branch, a tree trunk.
Light beckons me to search it out and follow.

A cloud formation appears as I look up from my preoccupation with a
book whose words I can now see.
In the clouds a figure of a goose in flight forms, giving affirmation
to me.

Yes, the Celts are right: the Spirit is like a wild goose going where it
wills, untamed, unfettered, calling,
"Trust! Come follow the impulse! Take wild flight! Ignore conformity's
will!"

Then I remember exactly where a key is hidden;
the key that unlocks the door to a familiar place.
It's where I searched before but was too impatient to find.
I hear a voice, You needed to spend time with Me, learning to trust what
is wild and free.

—Trudy Gomez

*For your reflection:* Have circumstances ever provided you the space
and time to spend with God?

246

*Mercy is a sweet gracious work of love, for mercy works in keeping us and turning to us all things for good. —Julian of Norwich*

## Mercy Moves Me

Mercy moves me
from places
where I get stuck,
places where
the need to fix
is so strong in me
that I believe I'm
the only one who
can make it right.

Mercy moves me
from clinging to
hurt or begrudging
another
to seeing the light
and essence
emanating from
the windows of
the soul.

Mercy moves me
steadily on my feet,
catches me before I trip
and skin my knees,
stops me in my tracks
before I gravely err
and can't turn back,
before I say what
cannot be unsaid.

Mercy moves me
when grace appears

right on time and
I let go of what has
a hold on me and
holds me back,
when my heart
softens just enough
for love to seep in.

Mercy moves me
when I lose my way
and need to be found.
Certain as the sunrise
faithfulness will find me.
Compassion, steadfast
and abundant, as droplets
of dew on blades of grass,
never fails.

Mercy moves me,
overcoming the
depths of darkness.
It's a transforming fire
that can never
be extinguished—
resurrection ushering
in a springtime
of redemption.

—Wendi Romero

*For your reflection:* Notice how mercy moves in your life.

*Make me to know your ways, O Lord. Teach me your paths.*
*Lead me in truth and teach me for you are the God of my Salvation.*
*—Psalm 25:4–5. He leads the humble in what is right, and teaches the*
*humble his way. —Psalm 25:9*

## Spirit Calling

What my eyes cannot see nor my mind understand, my heart opens
to suggestions by the spirit. Here at the pulse center, she waits for my
response to her call. I lean in on understanding which repeatedly seems
a great leap of faith. After silence and reflection, I begin to step forward
to her call. Truth unfolds, flooding a path through my veins, each cell
alive and moving toward goodness and wholeness. Once again, clarity
emerges. Peace encircles me, and I release to what is possible. My soul
renews to this purpose again and again. This calling has me returning to
its prompting, which constantly lies in wait.

—Gina Bradley

*For your reflection*: Sit in Silence. Listen with your heart? What is spirit
calling you to?

## Touchstones and Foundation Stones

God makes His presence known—
There are dwelling places where I meet God
Touchstones where I feel God's presence.
Early morning on the back deck
My home church when no one else is there
Moonlit nights when everything is quiet
Soaking in a tub of water.
The circle of my meditation/prayer group
Sharing a meal and laughter with family or friends
Early morning as I read scripture
Meditation time
Lying on a blanket in the back pasture, just being.
I have little altars around the house.
It may look like clutter to some;
For me they are sacred touchstones.
Bird feathers found on paths
Seashells from beaches where I experienced sunrise "church"
Stones from a mountain and creeks
Pictures of loved ones
A clay sculpture I made
My grandmother's holy water font
Other ephemera gathered
Things I arrange and rearrange.
These touchstones are endless.
I know deep within that God is everywhere and always present,
In the tangible touchstones and meeting places.
I know that God's kingdom is within.
I abide in God and God abides in me.
I am a dwelling place.
I am a portable altar,
A meeting place, a prayer space.
I don't always tend that altar,
I am not always present,

But God is ever faithful, ever present;
My Touchstone, my Foundation Stone.

—Trudy Gomez

***For your reflection***: Namaste, I bow to the divine in you, I acknowledge
that the Holy Spirit who dwells in me dwells in you.

*The Diffuse Shining of God is Hagia Sophia. Sophia is Gift, is Spirit,
Donum Dei. She is God-given and God Himself as Gift. Sophia in all
things is the Divine Life reflected in them.* —Thomas Merton

## Sophia, Gift, Spirit

We knew you well
before you were lost to us.
Before you became
the male spirit
no longer
whispering of birthing.

We knew you
as we know
our ordinary actions
of discerning and breath.
We knew you as the
inner guidance to Life.

I desire to have you
come close to me,
again as you were
in the beginning of time.
Close as the whisper
advocating for incarnation.

I will ponder with you.
I will reflect on
your presence
as it has always been
and the Truth to be
found as a body prayer.

Sophia of our heart,
at the beginning
of time,

You were there.
And you blew your breath
and birthed the waters.

—Avis Lyons LeBlanc

*For your reflection*: What do you feel when you ponder the breath of Hagia Sophia?

*Inspired by words in an e-mail from a dear friend, Diane,"Made me think of all that I can still be and was made to be." It was in response to reading my poem, "Freedom's Key." My muse spoke to me in in a deep southern drawl, so imagine and hear that voice as you read.*

## Potential Energy

Even at my age there is potential.
There is a law of physics that talks of potential energy:
energy that is stored up,
dammed up waiting to pour out,
coiled up waiting to spring forth.
Whatever expression it takes
whether its creates chaos or beauty,
it can be difficult to experience
it can make others uncomfortable.

That potential for change
whereby aspects of myself come forth,
aspects that I may not even have acknowledged
as a part of myself; aspects that change the way
I relate to others, the way others experience me.

That potential to change or transform relationships,
to make me wonder why not and others to ask why?
Most folks don't like change, it makes them uncomfortable
and unsure.

You become a person who is not the one they know;
except that potential energy was always there,
and somehow you are conscious of it.
It was there just waiting, waiting so long that it
had to burst from you like that stored divine energy
that caused the big bang.

The potential energy that has all that I can be,
that storehouse of energy of what I am made to be
waiting …

for its release.

—Trudy Gomez

*For your reflection*: Are you aware of your storehouse of potential
energy and are you ready to release your potential into the universe?

*Love is stronger than death. —Song of Solomon 8:6*

**Things Beyond Explaining**

Our nephew, Paul Lormand, was almost my age. My husband, Dee, is the youngest of a large family, and because of this has nieces and nephews not so much younger than he is. We have been very close to Paul; he was our son Jacques's godfather.

Paul was generous, humorous, and so interesting to talk to. He managed a college theater for years. He and I liked to talk about plays, movies, and books. He continued giving my son Jacques birthday and Christmas presents, far beyond the time (age 18 or so) when most godparents stop.

Paul moved to Kaplan with his son, Joseph, a teenager, in 2017. He was a single parent who was experiencing ill health, and he needed help from his sisters. In fact, his severe diabetes caused the loss of a leg not so long after he arrived. He rallied though, and got a prosthesis, and drove again, often visiting us or going to Lafayette and returning to our house with gumbo, jambalaya, or po boys that he had picked up. He loved coffee, and we made sure to have a pot for him. We always talked and laughed.

This story takes a tragic turn, because Paul contracted Covid-19 just after Thanksgiving of 2020. In fact, Thanksgiving dinner was the last time Dee, Jacques, or I would see him. There's a whole lesson wrapped up in that alone — that we just never know when we might last see someone.

Paul fought valiantly in intensive care for many months, until, finally, he passed away in June of 2021. He died on a Sunday, and I got the news the next day.

At this time, I was in Utah on a yoga and hiking retreat. On that Sunday evening, we were in a darkened room experiencing a guided meditation, followed by a head massage. The presenter, Amy, came to me first, as I lay on my yoga mat, and gently massaged my head. Then she moved to the next person. Then...I couldn't explain the fact that I now felt hands pressed gently on each side of my head. With the presence of these hands came a feeling of deep peace and contentment. I tried to move my eyes to see if Amy had come back to me, but I could hear her moving elsewhere in the quiet room. I didn't want those hands to go away. I lay as still as I could as my mind continued to wonder what was happening. After what seemed like a long time, the feeling of the hands gently left. I would find out the next day that Paul had died on this night, about an hour before. If he could have, he would have come to see about me. I think he did.

—Lyn Holley Doucet

*For your Reflection:* Many people have had mystical experiences that they have not shared with others. Perhaps you have had things happen that can't be explained in normal ways. Write about one such experience.

# This Day, This Moment

Photo by Denise Broussard

**Present Moment**

Follow the winding path
Explore awareness
Take the time
Be present in each step
Be present to the moment
Listen to the voice that says
Stop!
See!
Listen!
Smell!
Feel!
Appreciate!

—Trudy Gomez

*For your reflection*: Practice dwelling in the present moment.

*I am grateful for what I am and have. My thanksgiving is perpetual.*
—*Henry David Thoreau*

## More Than Enough

Abandoned chairs left at different angles,
half-empty glasses of melted ice water,
smeared lipstick lining a few rims of
finished wine goblets, and the French bread,
having shed its golden-brown skin,
left a meandering trail of scattered tidbits
from the life we shared at the table
to where the last philosophical thought
had been expressed. The butter dish
with a small, rounded knife, smeared with
the color of melted sun, laid resting on its side.

Just moments ago, flickering candles illuminated
faces and food around the table, warming
the conversation too; hardened wax from
the whoosh of breath extinguishing the flames
now sticks to the tablecloth. Linen napkins
crumpled up and left in disarray; plates
containing remnants from a meal
that took countless hours to prepare.
Pleasure and relief simultaneously
share a deep space within me now, as warm
water begins to fill the kitchen sink.

How many meals have been shared
and forgotten through the years?
Thoughts drift back to the beginning of
this day, agreements made to not talk of
politics or what divides us. Journeys of
hundreds of miles brought us to
this meal; the door opening to sounds of
laughter and the smell of roasting turkey,

loved ones rushing into one another's arms;
hugs that gather us in for no other reason than
to give thanks; board and card games played
while we wait for the meal.

As we play and eat, we reminisce
about generations before us, passing down
their oral history to their great-grandchildren.
It's the grandchildren who lead us back
to who we really are: their unconditional love,
their joy, their freedom of having no expectations.
They abide in the present surrounded by those
who love them. *This* is more than enough.

—Patty Prather

***For your reflection***: List five small things that you're grateful for and
may sometimes overlook in your daily life.

## Journeying

A voice calls, "Step out of your safe house."
Do I dare heed that call?
Do I trust enough to accept the invitation,
Surrender and be changed!

Step into places unimagined and unplanned
Stumbling on journey
Three step forward, two steps back
Shadow places
Wide open spaces
Rugged terrains
Along paths that challenge to the core.

Do I drag baggage behind me, burdening?
Do I cast the unneeded aside and dance the journey?
Back around in a circular path until lessons learned
Upward and onward
Taking opportunities
Running
Stepping gently

Fuel myself with Daily Bread,
Recognize Angels on the way,
Keep my eye on the Divine,
Listen to Spirit,
Allow myself to step into Mystery

—Trudy Gomez

*For your reflection:* How do you answer the call to *step out*?

*Place me like a seal over your heart, like a seal on your arm; for love is as strong as death. —Song of Songs 8:6*

## Mourning and Dancing

Watching a sunrise,
a beautiful light show
of brilliant red, orange,
and yellow colors.

Listening to doves cooing,
soothing and quieting
my troubled thoughts.
I ponder this morning.

Welcoming all.
The sights,
the sounds,
the silence.

Experiencing
grief and laughter,
love and hate,
sadness and gladness.
They belong together.

Life and love
are not possessing
just one thing,
one feeling,
or any one person.

Life and love
are about letting go,
seeing the gifts

in all things,
feelings, and people.

There is a time
for everything
under heaven.
Everything belongs,
all has a purpose.

Life and love
teach me to relax,
enjoy the sounds
of the mourning doves
in their dance.

Be still, breathe in,
breathe out.
Embrace the dawn,
a new beginning
of hope and awakening.

Accepting this moment,
knowing Christ is with me
in all of my life—
Loving me, here, there,
everywhere.

Love is stronger than death.
Love truly never dies.

—Denise Broussard

*For your reflection*: It takes two. Two dancers. Two souls. Two opposites. And can you accept that from two, God makes one beautiful union?

## Precipice

I stand on a precipice
my feet frozen in place,
a place of fear.

Deep breath, deep breath…
open my mind,
see with third eye.

I stand on a precipice,
toes curled,
a place of holding.

Deep breath, deep breath,
heart afire,
desire enkindled.

I stand on a precipice
one step away;
a place of uncertainty.

Deep breath, deep breath,
trust what you've learned,
the things discerned.

I stand on the precipice
hearing Love call
Come see! Come, see!

Deep breath, deep breath,
Step into hope,
fall into Mercy

—Trudy Gomez

*For your reflection*: What keeps you from answering the call, Come
see! Come, see! What do you need to release, and what do you need to
embrace, to answer Love's call?

*When one seeks love and connection with a desperate need.*

## Full Moon Eyes

I read,
"Everyone you see,
you say to them,
Love me."

The truth in that statement.
is felt the world over.
For me, I want to
transform that statement,
live a new statement.

And I say,
"let me love you."

I open to the glory and grace
surrounding me,
the care my partner gives to me,
the joy of living choice,
the friendships I enjoy.

And I say,
"let me love you."

Looking at life,
with love that
surrounds everything;
offering peace if we receive,
offering peace if we see anew,
And I say,
"let me love you."

Let me love
as bright and beautiful as

the shining of
the full moon.

From seeing the darkness
"do you love me?"
to attaining the light,
sharing the light,
"let me love you."

As I look upon
all that I see,
all that shows up
in the beauty of my life,
I want to look with new eyes.

Full Moon Eyes.

And I say,
"let me love you,
and I accept
that you love me."

—Avis Lyons LeBlanc

*For your reflection:* Just for today I will look with the light of love on my world and those I encounter.

*Natural awareness is luminous mind. —Diana Winston*

## Silent Sun

Silent sun, you are appearing,
Lifting salmon arms across the sky.
Silently you rise into forgetting,
and remembering this moment
we call time.

Silent sun, you are the heart of living,
and yet you rise not hurried, never forced.
I would like to live this lovely giving,
the ways you bring your warmth without reward.

Silent sun. The light shines clear with every breath.
And as the sky expands, your silence rings.
And now ... one mockingbird begins to sing.

— Lyn Holley Doucet

*For your reflection:* Watch the sunrise or sunset. Write your own poem.
Or draw with crayons.

# Transitions and Truths

Photo by Trudy Gomez

*One's destination is never a place, but a new way of seeing things.*
*—Henry Miller*

## My Turning Road

As I approach
this next turn
that is
the journey
of my life,
may I have
no fear
for I am
being led.

May the road
be kind and
gentle to me,
may it never
be sharp.
May the road
reveal itself
to me
with love.

May it never
be rude.
May the road
provide
all I will
ever need.
May it
always
be generous.

On my turning
road,
may I know
that I'm never
lost but merely
at a bend
where a new vista
waits to open
just for me.

—Wendi Romero

*For your reflection*: May you be open to new vistas.

*He makes the winds His messengers, flaming fire His ministers.*
*—Psalm 104:4*


### The Winds of Change

In the midst of blustering winds, questions swirl about me.
Tree limbs sway, leaves fly, time stands still.

Open mind. Open heart. Open soul.

Wanting, waiting, searching, knowing His Presence is here within.
Waiting to follow where Spirit leads.

Wintry winds are blowing, making a way for something new.
Leaves fall, trees naked, ground covered, soaked.

Preparing, nourishing earth for future growth.
What will 70 bring?

I will trust in Him.

—Velma LeBlanc Cheramie

*For your reflection*: Do you foresee coming times of change in your life? Will you allow the angels to guide you through these changes? Can this be another opportunity to learn to trust Him?

*Change isn't always easy. We sometimes grieve for what is no more. We fear, sometimes for nothing, for what's ahead. Moving from one situation to another is all about accepting what is, in this present moment.*

## Transitions

In the beginning she thought
she was a fatherless child.
Jesus said, "See what great love
the Father has lavished on us,
that we should be called
children of God!" (1 John 3:1)
She accepted His love.

Early on, she was a victim,
carrying guilt and shame.
Jesus said, "That we should be
holy and blameless before Him
in love." (Ephesians 1:4)
She survived.

At a young age, she was left a widow.
God said, "I am a defender
and have a special place
in my heart for the orphans
and fatherless and widows." (Psalm 146:9)
She trusted that she was
being "held by something larger
than her circumstances." (Paula D'Arcy)

In midlife, she didn't think
she had any gifts or talents.
But Jesus said, "We all have
different gifts.
If it is serving let him
serve others." (1 Peter 4:10)
She became a caregiver.

Her life was filled with trauma
and adversities. He said,
"Consider it pure joy
whenever you face trials
of many kinds." (James 1:2–4)
She finally came to realize
she was being prepared.

For great love and great suffering,
both are natural gateways
to spiritual transition and growth.
She accepted all of it,
letting Him take her
through all transitions
in her precious life.

—Denise Broussard

***For your reflection***: Can we just say a prayer of thanksgiving for what was and have hope for the future, and accept our precious lives to their fullest in the present?

*God of compassion, comfort us.*

## The Spiritual Chalkboard

What is it like not to see
and be in the darkness?
Does light peek in
to keep fear out?

No wonder loud noises
are disturbing.
Where are they coming from?
What do they mean?

I'm watching my friend
drift away … my friend
is dying, lying in the world
of in-between.

This brilliant mind that taught
so many to be educators,
now destroyed by some
disease invading her brain.

She seems to rest in confusion.
The sounds of voices
are familiar, appearing to
bring her comfort.

In your search for that place
of peace and understanding,
my friend, I pray you discover
this Greater Love that is forever.

She begins to have a conversation
when all alone, not for our ears
but for those inviting her
to the other side.

She's intent on trying to
comprehend the message received.
After listening carefully, she lifts
her hand up in the air.

She begins to write as though on
a chalkboard, the loyal teacher
that she was for so many years
taking notes of her final lesson.

Our voices seem to interrupt her.
It appears she is moving now
to a new place of learning,
her eternal classroom.

—Pat Low

*For your reflection*: Where do you find comfort in times of sorrow?

## Shepherd Me O God

I participated in the Advent Labyrinth walk in the garden of a local hospital. My intention: help me handle the stress of preparing for Christmas and help me remember the true meaning of Christmas in the midst of all the hoopla. I set this intention as I entered the labyrinth.

There are dedication bricks surrounding the labyrinth; as I navigated the labyrinth, one of them appeared in my line of sight. Inscribed on it was a little blurb that had the word, *shepherd,* in it (I can't remember the exact words, nor could I find that particular brick again) and I heard the words, *"Let me shepherd you."*

A few steps later, the phrase *"learn the lesson and move on"* came into my line of vision and stuck in my mind. My journey within the labyrinth seemed to become more effortless, my steps steady with these words of advice. When I reached the center of the labyrinth, a brisk wind was blowing and the cypress trees shivered and bent in the wind. *"When you walk with me you may bend, but you will not break."*

As I journeyed outward, I had to step aside and allow some of my fellow travelers space to journey ... *"Sometimes you have to step aside from what you are doing, from your expectations and allow: allow others to be who they are, allow things to unfold, pause, wait, allow, learn the lesson and move on."* This is possible if I allow myself to be shepherded, allow myself to be carried by my Shepherd.

—Trudy Gomez

*For your reflection:* Your ways, O LORD, make known to me; teach me your paths, guide me in your truth and teach me, for you are God my savior ... All the paths of the LORD are kindness and constancy toward those who keep his covenant and his decrees. The friendship of the LORD is with those who fear him, and his covenant, for their instruction. Ps.25:4-5a,8-9,10,14

*There, but for the grace of God, go I. —John Bradford*

## There, But for the Grace of Awakening, Go I

Like a lover longing for intimacy, awakening woos me.
Awakening reaches into my slumbering self through a
network of internal and external paths and loops.

Through dreams, nudging my unconscious to awaken;
through an embrace, a touch, a kind gaze, disarming
my defensive heart.

Through a story, a musical, a song, consoling painful
memories; through prayer and a heartfelt listener,
reconciling peace emerges from within.

Through creative endeavors, possibilities for my wholeness
are unveiled.

In times of colorful chaos and times of ordered boredom, awakening
listens within me to the silence of my inner abyss as the voice beneath
the silence garners her courage and steps into the radiance of her
awakened, authentic self.

—Elsa Diana Mendoza

*For your reflection*: How has the grace of awakening been revealed
to you?

# True Self and True Being

Photo by Trudy Gomez

## The Evolving You

I am the mother giving birth
to this new creation of me each day.
I am sustained by the Holy Mystery
with each breath and invited to participate
in this co-creation.

It is a delight to be so aware of this evolution.
Each moment I may see a new expression of
the mystery of me. The process of co-creation
to the ever new: me—You, You—me,
always feels like a beginning.
What an amazing journey.

—Betty Landreneau

*For your reflection*: Our choices direct the trajectory of our co-creation.
Which of your choices make you more aware of this process?

*It is only with the heart that one can rightly see.*
—*Antoine de St.-Exupery*


**It Takes a Whole Heart**

Some things remain
hidden from the mind
but known only
to the heart.

The mind is a warehouse,
storing what we think
we know and not knowing
what we don't.

Hiding is natural
when what longs
to be forgotten
is begging for attention,

but shadows are keepers
of our memories,
trailing the light and
following wherever we go.

Hidden from thought
are the mysteries of the heart,
things the mind can
never know.

It takes undeniable strength
and courage to embrace
both light and dark.
It takes a whole heart.

—Wendi Romero


***For your reflection***: What do you know deep in your heart that can't be
known any other way?

*Somewhere, something incredible is waiting to be known.*
*—Carl Sagan*

## Ode to Juno and Jupiter

To Rome, you are god of the heavens.
To Juno, you are beloved.

Moving in and out,
Juno skirts your mighty magnetism
with her titanium soul.
One wrong move and the lovers' dance
turns to fiery death.

Only she can bring your
majestic beauty into focus
where God's paintbrush
goes Van Gogh.

Your indigo poles swirling with storms.
Your belly heaving with hot hydrogen.
Juno knows there is more under the surface.

Intimacy gives her a glimpse of
ammonia rising below your cloud cover
discovering mysteries you are ready to reveal.

O, Juno and Jupiter,
may your celestial embrace
inspire your Earthly neighbors
to discover their own mysteries within.

—Michelle Lafleur MacFadyen

*For your reflection*: How will you make your true self known to a
loved one?

Note: In Roman mythology, Juno is the wife of Jupiter. As a NASA space probe, Juno has been wedded to Jupiter since 2016. To see her latest discoveries and photos that inspired this piece, go to www.nasa.gov/mission_pages/juno

After completing her mission, Juno will plunge into Jupiter's atmosphere for their final dance.

*An authentic life is the most personal form of worship and is the soul made visible. — bj King*

## Be Your Beautiful Self

My dear friend, mentor, and teacher, bj King, recently shared this personal quote and it had the power to stop me in my tracks. How profound a thought that we could honor our Creator in the deepest, most intimate and personal way by merely living our life in a way that reflected our purest personal imprint. That of our soul…our very essence. because when we live our life in alignment with our SOUL, we are expressing ourselves in the way that God intended! We each have a unique imprint! And when we are living a life reflecting our "unique soul imprint", we will know it because we will feel ALIVE, HAPPY, FULFILLED, AND INSPIRED … This is a truth!!!!

So what does that mean for you and I, on a daily basis? Have the dreams and yearnings I have not yet fulfilled left a vacant spot in my "authentic life"? My feeling is … yes. We are always changing and growing, so what might be authentic at age 20 might not (and probably won't be) what feels authentic at 50. But how do we know what our soul is asking of us? Consider what brings you joy and satisfaction. Also things that might come easily to you. Watch what catches your eye, your mind and elevates you and inspires you. THIS is your soul in action. Speaking to you.

One can connect to our highest self, our soul, by asking GOD/Our higher self that we be in communication our Soul at all times. With it, and only it. As humans, we are bombarded daily by information outside of ourselves that influences how we think, act and feel. Others feelings, thoughts and emotions, the media, newspapers, social media, politics, and idea platforms of all kinds. As our thoughts hinge on these things the energy then grows and begin to influence us without us even noticing. Then we begin to feel … "Off."

When we allow something OUTSIDE OF OURSELF to dictate what goes on INSIDE OF OURSELF we begin to break away from our authenticity. Each day, ask that you be guided only by the highest level of your soul and see what happens! Allow yourself to say "no" to things that you are not guided to authentically. Allow yourself to say "no" to clothing that no longer suits you. Allow yourself to say "no" to people, places and things that do not feel "right." This is so critical to not blur or distort our perception and decisions. This is your soul speak- ing to you.

Of course, doing our own personal work is critical so that we can clear old patterns, distortions and blocks that we have developed over our lifetime of trying to maneuver our way through life. There is no judgement as these were survival mechanisms. But, these things can hinder you from acting on your soul's impulse. Fear, insecurity, defense tactics—they will take you away from that which is yours and from the JOY that living authentically can bring..

NOW is the time to agree to live life on your own terms…that which is your birthright from our Creator. Your authentic life reflecting your own personal soul imprint. Could there be anything more beautiful? I truly believe this is one of the great secrets of life, and what God truly wants for each of us.

BE YOUR BEAUTIFUL SELF.

—Ann Kergan

*For your reflection:* How can I live my life more authentically so that I am in alignment with my true soul imprint and through that honor God and my Authentic Self?

*Several years ago, I was invited to a wedding and I experienced such angst as to what I would wear. This was so unlike me and, at the time, I questioned the bigger picture of what was happening. The wedding date arrived, and as I sat in the church surrounded by guests, I noticed how each woman had on a unique dress. Like the women wearing them, they were such lovely and diverse dresses. The beginnings of the piece below came to me.*

### Dresses at the Wedding

Some wore red, some wore black, some blue, some yellow, some purple or green short-sleeved or sleeveless, despite the chill of a crisp autumn evening. Lace, satin, wool, and the styles—more than you can imagine. Each cut in a different way yet each as beautiful and unique as the woman wearing it.

Aren't we, as individual women, all different and lovely in our own way? Is one better than the other? I think not, but therein lies the problem: I think! It is only our human judgment that deems one dress prettier than another just as we, seeing only with the eyes of our mind, decide that one woman is smarter, better, more perfect than another.

There is beauty in our differences. Just as each dress is a beautiful piece of art in its own right, we women are all individuals, strong and beautiful in our own right.

At times I need to be reminded to look with the eyes of my heart and not the judgment of my mind. To quote Alice Walker: "In nature, nothing is perfect and everything is perfect. Trees can be contorted, bent in weird ways, and they're still beautiful."

—Lissee Spiller

***For your reflection:*** Lord, give me the grace to stop and look with the eyes of my heart, that I may find the beauty in all things and people.

*A picture is worth a thousand words, as the adage goes. But the pictures aren't accurate representations of our true reality.*
—*Fred Barnard*

## A Picture-Perfect Life

I can't count the times my children and I have heard this statement, "Oh, it must be so nice to have a picture-perfect life." I've had to explain how that comment used to really bother me. After the traumas and tragedies I've experienced in my past, I totally understand how it might make them feel when that line is repeated to them. They too, have gone through their own adversities, and the road hasn't always been an easy one.

Other words that used to make me feel uncomfortable years ago are: "You are so strong, and God never gives us more than we can handle." These statements just made me feel worse at times. I would think if God was sending me these losses and tragedies because I was so strong, then I didn't want to be. To be very honest, I got really tired of hearing those comments, because I didn't know my own strength through Christ in those early years.

With time, prayer, silence, scripture-reading, I came across a verse in Corinthians that spoke to me. I'm guessing it came to me when I was finally ready. "No testing has overtaken you that is not common to everyone. God is faithful, and he will not let you be tested beyond your strength, but will also provide the way out so that you may be able to endure it." 1 Corinthians 10:13.

In my heart, I never worshiped a punishing God, but a forgiving and loving Father. My feelings about this verse are very simple. Life, not God, sends adversity to us, and then He provides love, strength, resources, and courage to endure and move forward. I believe He allows it since He has given us all free will, free choice, and ultimately when we choose to turn towards Him, an understanding of the lessons learned.

When I finally accepted that God was giving me the strength to always push forward, I welcomed those comments and started giving

Him all the glory. He says, "That is why, for Christ's sake, I delight in weaknesses, in insults, in hardships, in persecutions, in difficulties. For when I am weak, then I am strong." 2 Corinthians 12:10

Remember, when speaking with anyone, look into their eyes, and listen to them. We have no idea where their life's journey has taken them; so we must choose our words wisely, know when to be silent, and just be there for them. Many times, I admit, even though I know what I know now, I've had diarrhea of the mouth; wishing later that I would have thought before I had spoken. I'm just as guilty, because I've been bothered by some of my own spoken words.

I shared with my children a few years ago that I realized that we should take those statements as a compliment, because through faith, we've been able to take our pain and suffering from our traumas to a level of grace and gift. We have become better human beings because of them.

I thank God that we don't live bitter and hateful lives, questioning "Why me?" Now I ask, "Why not me?" Because of our trust in Him, we don't constantly dwell on it, but it's always there. Our bodies never forget. People who make those comments might not know what else to say. They could be wounded themselves, still holding their own pain deep inside, or simply attempting to make you feel better. When we are still hurting, have yet to meet our pain and recover, is when we take offense.

Yes, we grieve. Yes, we hurt. Yes, we cry. But we don't blame others for our losses, and we live our precious lives to the fullest no matter what, as He wants us to. I believe our task on earth is to find the true, the good, and the beautiful in everything, even in the darkest situations. I've chosen to walk forward into the light of each new day as long as I am able.

Believe me, we have known darkness, as so many others have. I just read this book again, When Bad Things Happen to Good People, which offers clear thinking and consolation in times of sorrow. It's life and how will we react to it?

Thank you Jesus, we have strong, loving souls with the holy spirit within each of us. Knowing this has helped us attain peace that only He could give, and nothing or no one can take it away unless we so choose. I have told my kids a million times, "There is light at the end of the tunnel, so keep pushing forward and never give up."

—Denise Broussard

*For your reflection*: Love is strong. Love will win. Can you be a testament to these statements? What do you choose to do with your trauma?

*How will you make your true self known to a loved one?*
—*Michelle Lafleur MacFadyen*

## Being Fully Known

This question offers us entry into an important reflection on how we present in the world. Do we contribute to humanity and, closer in, to our community? Even closer, do we contribute to our own care and positive evolution and those of a loved one?

As always, a journal is a tremendous support in developing our reflections. We often have very good insights or ideas that we think we will remember but that pass away as those wispy dreams we plan to remember in the morning. Write them down.

My own reflection brings me to making my true self known to me. I am often unaware of how or what I feel about things in any given moment. I just, by rote, go through my day unaware of my experiences and my reactions to thoughts and happenings. I know this all goes back to being here now and present moment stuff. Difficult for us all I think but something we are mostly aware of and something we mostly forget to do.

I think the method of The Examen, presented in Ignatian Spirituality, of observing your day in the presence of God in thankful reflection on where God is in your everyday life is very helpful in keeping us more present. This reflection helps us to see if our thoughts, beliefs, and attitudes add joy to our day or if we need to make some corrections. Making this a prayer and meditation at the end of the day can help us enter sleep time with a clear mind and heart.

I also like to start my day with ideas of how I want to feel today. I want joy, so what do I need to bring into my life to feel joyful today? I would like a sense of accomplishment when it is time to do The Examen. How can I structure my day to create the accomplishment? I know I need to add more physical activity if I am going to feel at all good about what I accomplished today. I know that the more joyful I am and the more I feel

I have contributed and accomplished some healthy activities, the more I will be able to recognize the presence of the Divine in my life.

Another tool that has proven helpful to me over the years is a gratitude journal. Writing the things I am grateful for and why I am grateful for them keeps me in a place of hope and a sense of life going in the right direction. I read somewhere that gratitude puts us in a miracle mind-set and I believe it is true. I find that speaking or writing gratitude, however small a piece you can find, about challenges we are having will offer miracles to the circumstance. I believe it.

The more I Examen, the more I will make my true self known to me. The more I create the delightful feelings and attitudes, the more I will be in the present moment because it is the happening place. The more grateful I am, the more miracles I open to.

—Avis Lyons LeBlanc

*For your reflection*: Find and employ those tools that help you become more present to your life and to Divine assistance.

# Wonder and Holy Pauses

Photo by Michelle Lafleur MacFadyen

*It has been said that non-human living things approach us to remind us of loved ones who have passed.*

## The Dragonflies

The dragonflies had flown around some of his loved ones at the baseball park days before his death. They would land on their hat brims, or on a shoulder or two. Later that week, after his passing, they were plentiful near the family pond. One grandchild giggled when she felt the flutter of the dragonfly's wings as it landed on her arm. She had heard us speak of the dragonflies in connection with him. She joyfully shouted, "Pa's here!" Another brave one touched her cheek. She chased it as it flew away!

That Easter, near the pond, at its edge, the dragonflies seemed to have descended upon all who were present on this Resurrection Day! There were many touching down on fingertips extended like landing pads. Many fluttered near others' cheeks as they stood motionless. All stood still to welcome them; we all had a sense that these were here to let us know our loved ones had come to visit!

— Cheryl Delahoussaye

*For your reflection*: Do some living things remind you of a loved one who has passed on?

*Holiness comes wrapped in the ordinary. There are burning bushes all around you. Every tree is full of angels.*
—Macrina Wiederkehr

### Angel in the Clouds

Long arms of fiery pink
like a roseate spoonbill
outstretched in flight
reach out to me.
She takes my dark
blue heart and lifts
it high so I might see
what she already knows.

"Hope trails alongside me
like a best friend,"
and death a companion,
not a fearful foe.
So I no longer fight
the natural order of things.
I was meant for
revelations such as these—

morning rays breaking
through the trees, a breeze
brushing my tear-soaked
cheek, a soft wind-song
playing in the chimes,
and pastel colors lifting
this aching heart of mine
across an evening sky.

—Wendi Romero

*quote by Macrina Wiederkehr

***For your reflection***: Become aware of the presence of angels.

## Sacred Science

The best part of becoming has been learning from folks in various stages and phases of professional and personal development. Dr Masgutova's Neurosensorimotor Reflex Integration, a mix between physical therapy, occupational therapy, speech therapy, and psycho-therapy, explores the biomechanics of the human experience through the lens of primitive reflexes.

This modality attracts the most lovely clinicians from around the world to provide integrative care that allows bodies to live their best lives or, as Dr. M says, maximize brain potential. As progressive professionals we all enjoy the inner workings of neurobiology, but for me this work will always be deeply spiritual. For me it is "the missing link" between science and spirituality.

A mentor and colleague often will exclaim the phrase "control the line" or "control your line" when working with the body's center gravity lines and motor coordinating systems. Although this is serious work, I chuckle on the inside every time, as these words fill the atmosphere in her polish-English dialect.

As I see it, these lines are God's presence creating our "place in space" or proprioception. We are wired to hold the line, to center our breath like children gathering at Momma's holiday table.

Each moment of centering alongside these wise women of Sacred Center is a coming home of sorts. We gather in a safe place to hold the line, giving honor to each of our "places in space." We sing over the bones thrown aside from the patriarchal influences of our modern society—without contempt but with the sweet fragrance of Momma's feast day desserts. We overflow and leak wordless pains and joys too, blessing the sacred ground that this "place in space" honors.

This proprioception that illuminates the nervous systems over all functionality is more than serious work; it is spiritual work that for me fortifies stress resilience. This centering, this serious spiritual work allows for freedom in ways we can only hope semantics can hold. But for those brave and vulnerable enough to just BE with this center gravity line, the tension loses its hold and ignites something wild and beautiful laid within conception.

I just love how we are wired for connection with the divine and how science confirms this recipe for freedom.

—Bridgette Mouton

*For your reflection*: In what ways do you see science and sacred connect?

*Beauty is eternity here below.* —*Simone Weil*
*I wrote this poem after a retreat during which a Luna Moth attached itself to my cabin.*

## Visitation

I see you and gasp with wonder.
You bring me to my knees in worship.
My throat fills with something like longing, something like
a longing-love.

You are so still; are you alive?
Tentatively I touch my pinkie finger to your wing, and you stir
but do not leave me.
Sacred visitor, messenger, moon-bearer.

You stay as moments drift upward like bubbles from a child's wand.
Silence. As your green shines vivid on the rusty wood
and I can't be still enough.
You stay until
there's no mistake.

You came for me.

—Lyn Holley Doucet

*For your reflection*: Has a certain aspect of nature or the sight of an animal entered your heart in a special way? Write about that today.

## Little Maroon Ribbon

It is the Sacred Center celebration of Mary Magdalene at a lovely home in Lafayette, La. I approach the labyrinth which is sheltered by old oaks and surrounded by fox-tail ferns. Warm and loving women have gathered to celebrate the Divine Feminine.

I walk the labyrinth path and along the way I see many shells, a rock with a red heart, stones and statues. A maroon ribbon that Lyn has placed on the labyrinth bids me to come closer. It is long and silky ... perfect for my flowing emotions and my readiness to just be. I pick it up and take off, skipping over the grass. The wind takes its weightless essence, allowing it to flow freely along with my thoughts. I am that young dancer moving gracefully, twirling effortlessly. On my body there are no restrictions! I AM! I SIMPLY AM.

With grace and courage I run, the ribbon spinning behind me as though I am shedding all that is holding me bound. Loosening my grip, letting go a little more, I wrap myself in the ribbon's safe embrace as it continues to tenderly hug my broken self, my shattered image. I hear, "You don't have to hold things together. A love which is weightless, flowing, and tender holds it for you. You can let it go now. You really can."

All of my life I have felt judged and found lacking. Something within me was healed by the flowing of my unconditional acceptance of myself as I danced with that ribbon. I tasted the freedom of just being me and being enough, just as I am.

Later I returned to the labyrinth and softly put the ribbon down, knowing it would bring solace and comfort to yet another! Thank you, my little maroon ribbon! I am grateful for this precious time. To be. To be me.

—Janice Richard

*For your reflection:* Pick up your little ribbon and just be you! How can you do that today?

*A Divine heart so merciful and kind that no wounding is possible. She never belittles, separates, or excludes. —Beverly Lanzetta*

## The Divine Feminine

It is evening in a rural Jewish village, all through the centuries. It is Friday evening and the people, mostly men, are finishing their work in the fields. The sun is close to setting. Bright streaks of color fill the sky.

They all begin to sing for her. They call her, "Shekinah. Come to us and be with us for Sabbath."

She is the sweetness of the Godhead, the approachable God, the glory of God. They invite her to the table. Later the women light the candles and move their hands over the flames. They invite the Holy to come to the table.

I close with this quote from Rabbi Jill Hammer: There is a Jewish custom to recite the poem Lecha Dodi, "Come, My Beloved"—on Friday night, as they turn to the door of the synagogue to greet the Sabbath. What most Jews don't know is that Jewish mystics regard the Sabbath as an embodiment of the immanent, feminine face of God.

Lecha Dodi: Come my Beloved. Beautiful One.

—Lyn Holley Doucet

*For your reflection:* Can you experience the Divine as so merciful and kind that no wounding is possible? Why or why not? Can you see God with a Mother's face? Why or why not?

*This is a poem I wrote at the Hayden Summer Dream Conference in North Carolina, after hearing her new poem read by Miribai Starr. My poem was first shared before we walked the labyrinth at our annual Mary Magdalene Celebration in 2022.*

## My Delight

Come, you dream makers,
You soul rakers,
Those who tend the fire of Her who walks in the world.
Fire keepers, eyes weeping, feet walking, hands lifting.

Come, you music makers, portrait painters, food givers,
Flower pickers ... Come ...
Dance!
Heart tenders, bodies fertile, soul lifters, truth seekers,
Time to dance and hold a space for rain,
For change,
For a new love ...
And a new world.

—Lyn Holley Doucet

***For your reflection:*** Is there a line of this poem that most speaks to you? Write it in your journal and spend some time thinking or writing about it.

## Acknowledgements

Thank you to Wendi Romero whose diligence, organizational skills, and managing of so many threads, has brought this book to fruition.

Much gratitude for Vinita Wright's grouping of our poems and essays according to themes. In each section, she took our individual writings and brought them to a meaningful whole.

The tedious work of further editing was taken on by Velma Leblanc Cheramie, Pat Low, Lissee Spiller, Patricia Drury Sidman, and Trudy Gomez. For your efforts, we are very grateful.

Deep gratitude to Avis Lyons LeBlanc who took on the difficult task of managing the manuscript from the beginning, through all of its changes, and bringing it to life in this book.

To Ann Kergan and Deidre Montgomery, for your generosity and gracious hospitality in hosting events for Sacred Center.

Gratitude to each of the Sacred Sisters who authored pieces for this book and to the ones who encouraged and supported its creation and development.

As always, Lyn Holley Doucet, thank you for your dedication to the dream that keeps this Center alive; supporting, comforting, bringing joy and sisterhood to all who show up.

Printed in the United States
by Baker & Taylor Publisher Services